TRADITIONS OF CHRISTIAN SPIRITUALITY

THE POETIC IMAGINATION

THE POETIC IMAGINATION

An Anglican Spiritual Tradition

L. WILLIAM COUNTRYMAN

SERIES EDITOR:
Philip Sheldrake

ORBIS BOOKS

Maryknoll, New York 10545

The Catholic Foreign Mission Society of America (Maryknoll) recruits and trains people for overseas missionary service. Through Orbis Books, Maryknoll aims to foster the international dialogue that is essential to mission. The books published, however, reflect the opinions of their authors and are not meant to represent the official position of the society. To obtain more information about Maryknoll and Orbis Books, please visit our website at www.maryknoll.org.

First published in 1999 by
Darton, Longman and Todd Ltd.
1 Spencer Court
140–142 Wandsworth High Street
London SW18 4JJ
Great Britain

Published in the USA in 2000 by
Orbis Books
P.O. Box 308
Maryknoll, New York 10545–0308
U.S.A.

Orbis ISBN 1–57075–307–5

Phototypeset in 10/13¼pt New Century Schoolbook
by Intype London Ltd
Printed and bound in Great Britain by
Redwood Books, Trowbridge, Wiltshire

Library of Congress Cataloging-in-Publication Data

Countryman, Louis William, 1941–
    The poetic imagination : an Anglican spiritual tradition / L. William Countryman.
        p.   cm.—(Traditions of Christian spirituality)
    Includes bibliographical references.
    ISBN 1–57075–307–5 (pbk.)
    1. English poetry—History and criticism.   2. English poetry—Anglican authors—History and criticism.   3. Christian poetry, English—History and criticism.   4. Christianity and literature—England—History.
5. Church of England—In literature.   6. Spirituality—Church of England.   7. Spirituality in literature.   I. Title.   II. Series.
PR508.R4   C67   2000
821.009′382—dc21   99–049300

for
Jon
who bore with the writer
and the writing

CONTENTS

PREFACE TO THE SERIES

Nowadays, in the western world, there is a widespread hunger for spirituality in all its forms. This is not confined to traditional religious people let alone to regular churchgoers. The desire for resources to sustain the spiritual quest has led many people to seek wisdom in unfamiliar places. Some have turned to cultures other than their own. The fascination with Native American or Aboriginal Australian spiritualities is a case in point. Other people have been attracted by the religions of India and Tibet or the Jewish Kabbalah and Sufi mysticism. One problem is that, in comparison to other religions, Christianity is not always associated in people's minds with 'spirituality'. The exceptions are a few figures from the past who have achieved almost cult status such as Hildegard of Bingen or Meister Eckhart. This is a great pity for Christianity East and West over two thousand years has given birth to an immense range of spiritual wisdom. Many traditions continue to be active today. Others that were forgotten are being rediscovered and reinterpreted.

It is a long time since an extended series of introductions to Christian spiritual traditions has been available in English. Given the present climate, it is an opportune moment for a new series which will help more people to be aware of the great spiritual riches available within the Christian tradition.

The overall purpose of the series is to make selected spiritual traditions available to a contemporary readership. The books seek to provide accurate and balanced historical and thematic treatments of their subjects. The authors are also conscious of the need to make connections with contemporary experience and values without being artificial or reducing a tradition to one dimension. The authors are well-versed in reliable scholarship about the traditions they describe. However, their intention is that the books should be fresh in style and accessible to the general reader.

One problem that such a series inevitably faces is the word 'spirituality'. For example, it is increasingly used beyond religious circles and does not necessarily imply a faith tradition. Again, it could mean substantially different things for a Christian and a Buddhist. Within Christianity itself, the word in its modern sense is relatively recent. The reality that it stands for differs subtly in the different contexts of time and place. Historically, 'spirituality' covers a breadth of human experience and a wide range of values and practices.

No single definition of 'spirituality' has been imposed on the authors in this series. Yet, despite the breadth of the series there is a sense of a common core in the writers themselves and in the traditions they describe. All Christian spiritual traditions have their source in three things. First, while drawing on ordinary experience and even religious insights from elsewhere, Christian spiritualities are rooted in the scriptures and particularly in the gospels. Second, spiritual traditions are not derived from abstract theory but from attempts to live out gospel values in a positive yet critical way within specific historical and cultural contexts. Third, the experiences and insights of individuals and groups are not isolated but are related to the wider Christian tradition of beliefs, practices and community life. From a Christian perspective, spirituality is not just concerned with prayer or even with narrowly religious activities. It concerns the whole of human life, viewed in terms of a conscious relationship with God, in Jesus Christ, through the indwelling of the Holy Spirit and within a community of believers.

The series as a whole includes traditions that probably would not have appeared twenty years ago. The authors themselves have been encouraged to challenge, where appropriate, inaccurate assumptions about their particular tradition. While conscious of their own biases, authors have nonetheless sought to correct the imbalances of the past. Previous understandings of what is mainstream or 'orthodox' sometimes need to be questioned. People or practices that became marginal demand to be re-examined. Studies of spirituality in the past frequently underestimated or ignored the role of women. Sometimes the treatments of spiritual traditions were culturally one-sided because they were written from an uncritical western European or North Atlantic perspective.

However, any series is necessarily selective. It cannot hope to do full justice to the extraordinary variety of Christian spiritual traditions. The principles of selection are inevitably open to question. I hope that an appropriate balance has been maintained between a sense of the likely readership on the one hand and the dangers of narrowness on the other. In the end, choices had to be made and the result is inevitably weighted in favour of traditions that have achieved 'classic' status or which seem to capture the contemporary imagination. Within these limits, I trust that the series will offer a reasonably balanced account of what the Christian spiritual tradition has to offer.

As editor of the series I would like to thank all the authors who agreed to contribute and for the stimulating conversations and correspondence that sometimes resulted. I am especially grateful for the high quality of their work which made my task so much easier. Editing such a series is a complex undertaking. I have worked closely throughout with Morag Reeve of Darton, Longman & Todd and Robert Ellsberg of Orbis Books. I am immensely grateful to them for their friendly support and judicious advice. Without them this series would never have come together.

PHILIP SHELDRAKE
Sarum College, Salisbury

ACKNOWLEDGEMENTS

Thanks are due to the following for permission to quote copyright material:

Faber & Faber Ltd for 'In Schrafft's', 'For the Time Being', 'Ascension Day, 1964', 'The Love Feast', 'Danse Macabre', 'The Shield of Achilles' and 'Whitsunday in Kirchsetten' by W. H. Auden; 'Little Gidding' and 'East Coker' from 'The Four Quartets' by T. S. Eliot, taken from *Collected Poems 1909–1962*; 'Who Is This Who Howls and Mutters' and 'The Airy Christ: After reading Dr Rieu's translation of St Mark's Gospel' by Stevie Smith, taken from *A Selection*.

HarperCollins Publishers for 'Night Herons', 'Child with a Dead Animal', 'Cyclone and Aftermath' and 'Prayer' by Judith Wright, taken from *Collected Poems*.

Macmillan Publishers Ltd for 'Arrival', 'A Country', 'Covenanters (Paul)', 'Suddenly after a long silence', 'In Church', 'Absence', 'Folk Tale' and 'This One' by R. S. Thomas, taken from *Collected Poems*.

New Directions Publishing Corp for 'The Parable of the Old Men and the Young', 'Soldier's Dream', 'The Kind Ghosts', 'Maundy Thursday' and 'Nocturne' by Wilfred Owen, from *The Collected Poems of Wilfred Owen*. Copyright © 1963 by Chatto & Windus, Ltd.

Tom Thompson for 'Grace', 'In Praise of Marriages', 'Reading Thomas Traherne', 'Request to a Year', 'Two Songs for the World's End' and 'Good News' by Judith Wright.

INTRODUCTION

To write about any topic of human importance generally involves falsifying it in one or more ways. Nowhere is this danger greater than with regard to the topic in hand here – the Anglican spirituality that comes to expression in lyric poetry. No aspect of it is without its problems of definition and understanding. Anglicanism is notorious for its theological indeterminacy. Spirituality is apt to speak of itself in images and riddles, while those who write about it often want to reduce it to something else: theology, philosophy, piety, politics or whatever. Poetry, in its turn, sometimes speaks of itself – but not often. And it has become the object of literary studies, written in expository prose, which sometimes seem more interested in the internal warfare of the guild of literary scholars than in returning the reader to the poetry itself with new insight.[1]

The problems are innate and essential to these subjects. Poetry is not concerned primarily with poetry, but with human experience of a larger world of feeling, value, encounter, interpretation, music, rhythm – all of which the poem takes up into itself in varying ways. The poet stands alongside the reader in contemplating and speaking of this larger world; the reader's view does not halt at the poem, but overlaps and goes beyond it and perhaps gains in perspective and definition through it. In a similar way, the great authors of spirituality do not speak primarily about spirituality itself, but about the Holy, the True, the Ultimately Real that we encounter in and through spirituality and that transforms us and our lives through our encountering it. Even Anglicanism exists in a mode unlike that of most Western Christian traditions. It has never been a genuinely confessional church. It is the product of historical accident (and/or divine providence) as much as of theological intent, and its primary focus is not on defining itself but on turning a community toward God in worship.

All three of the phenomena that intersect in the subject of this book – poetry, spirituality, Anglicanism – are vastly articulate, but not in describing or defining themselves. The question, then, arises how to write a book that will try to explain or interpret their intersection without somehow committing violent distortion on them all, individually and collectively. What, for that matter, do we mean by 'explain or interpret'? In the academic world, such terms typically mean that one will subject some object of study to analysis, decomposition, an alien evaluation of what is important in it and what not, and the reconstitution of select elements in a structure predetermined by the chosen academic discipline of reference and its favoured modes of discourse. Do we really succeed in interpreting or explaining only when we have translated our subject matter into a discourse alien to it? Or is it possible to remain closer to the source, as it were, and to present an account 'from within' that will be sufficiently aware of its own presuppositions and limitations to be accessible to others?[2]

Certainly, in our multicultural world, it is vital to explain and interpret one's own tradition in terms intelligible to others. It may, however, be equally vital for us to interpret our traditions to ourselves. Our multiculturalism, after all, is something that resides not merely in the total population, but in smaller, apparently more homogeneous communities and even inside each individual, formed as we are by an age of rapid travel and communication. The tradition under study was rooted in a very different world. For centuries, Anglicanism was simply the dominant form of Christianity in England. It was, for the most part, simply the 'unmarked' version of Christian faith – what modern computer terminology calls the 'default option'. It required little in the way of particular distinctives, and it had limited need to explain itself to others. It will require great care and tact, if one is to begin doing so today.

In any case, a living human tradition should always be free to suggest its own terms of understanding. In the present work, I write from within a horizon shared by Anglicans in whose spirituality English lyric poetry occupies a significant place. In other words, I shall be writing about a canon – a collection of literature defined less by its authors than by its readers (though, to be sure, its authors have also been readers of their predecessors). I shall be interested less in the individual poet and poem than in how they suggest, when read together, a certain perspective on life in the presence of God.

Behind this literary canon stands a community, both in the sense that a community has defined the canon and also in the sense that a community provides the context in which the individual pieces of the canon have arisen. If the poets offered us a purely literary kind of spirituality, it would be of limited interest. But, in fact, their work arises out of and addresses a spiritual tradition that can also be corroborated from the lives of people who may never read poetry at all. Even those who do read this canon do not, typically, turn to it primarily in order to learn this spirituality, as if it had to be brought into one's life from outside; they turn to it for companionship in practising what they have already begun to understand of life in the presence of the Holy.

I have some positive goals in writing this work. I hope that those who already know and love this canon will be able to recognise it in this work and even perhaps find something new and useful to them. I also hope that people of other traditions will here find the opportunity to share this perspective, even if in a brief and limited way – the odd and surprising opportunity to see life and the Holy through another set of eyes. I also have some negative goals. I hope to avoid over-defining something that is in fact resistant to definition. The subject calls for a certain fluidity and open-endedness in any treatment of it. Accordingly, I shall not suggest an overall structure nor offer a detailed analysis nor a step-by-step introduction to it, but point to a series of fundamental elements that pervade the tradition in a variety of forms and with changing emphases. I shall also endeavour to point the reader back always to the poetry itself rather than offering a freeze-dried prose substitute for it. When all is said and done, this tradition of spirituality will never be caught successfully except in the words of the poetry itself.

In my selection of poets, I have kept close, on the whole, to major figures – the sort of poets whose work is frequently anthologised. I have allowed myself to add Judith Wright, who is sadly little known in the United States.[3] Any lover of poetry will have a list of others whom I ought to have included. I will begin the list here myself by expressing my regrets at omitting Henry King, Edith Sitwell, and a number of nineteenth- and twentieth-century poets who seem at home in this tradition of spirituality even though they had no particular Anglican connection, especially Emily Dickinson.

I have drawn the quotations of poems from the odd assortment of editions that stock my own well-thumbed library, despite a lingering sense of shame that I have not searched out the best critical editions. But in the works of earlier poets, I have modernised spelling and punctuation rather freely.

Biblical quotations are from the Authorised (or King James) Version of the Bible. Given its long dominance and its role in shaping the English language, there seemed no choice in the matter; and I have enjoyed discovering afresh how much better it is than most of its successors.

My thanks to Philip Sheldrake for urging me to write this book, despite my repeated protests that it was not a job for a New Testament scholar. May the reader of it gain even a small portion of what I have received in writing it!

1. A POETIC SPIRITUALITY

SPIRITUALITY AND THE ENGLISH LYRIC POEM

Spiritualities flourish in face-to-face conversation, the arena of the spoken word, where counsel is given and received, the arena where people who have found themselves, perhaps quite against their own preferences, living in the presence of the divine Mysteries seek each other out in the hope of sharing the task of priestly discernment and understanding.[1] There is an element in spirituality that is always individual and contingent, always of the specific and unrepeatable moment; in this regard, spirituality can only belong to the oral context, the moment of here and now. But spiritualities also have a propensity for embodying themselves in writing. They have given rise to innumerable volumes of many sorts: books of spiritual direction, of meditations, of advice, of 'rules and exercises', of ascetical exhortation, of sermons, of allegories, of descriptions of what it is like to live on the border of the Holy, of impossible attempts to express the inexpressible experience of Union. Most of these are in prose, some in poetry. Many of these works have retained a readership over a long period of time. Some have even entered into the literary canon of their language, as has the English lyric poetry that provides the main focus of this study.

The use of lyric as a vehicle for spiritual discourse is not unique to the English language or to the Anglican tradition. One need think only of such authors as Simeon the New Theologian or John of the Cross to recognise this. The poetic imagination has, however, been particularly characteristic of Anglican spirituality. A study of Anglican spirituality therefore gives us a good occasion to think about the nature of spirituality and of the poetic imagination as manifest in lyric poetry. What about each of them makes lyric a suitable literary vehicle for a particular kind of spiritual discourse? What are the opportunities that lyric offers and the limitations that go along with them? What in the nature of spirituality most readily finds expression through the poetic imagination?

'Spirituality' is a word to which we can ascribe many different meanings. There is some agreement that it refers to the aspect of human experience and reflection concerned pre-eminently with meaning and values and with each person's living participation in them. Beyond that, there is plenty of room for disagreement. This is hardly the place to try to settle the question once and for all, but the reader would probably like to have at least a preliminary sense of what the present author means when he uses the term. I should say that spirituality resides, decisively, in the individual person, where it forms an inner and consensual relationship with Ultimate Truth or Absolute Reality or God or whatever metaphor one uses to name that Mystery that lies at the foundation of all that is.[2] I do not mean, by referring to 'the individual person', that spirituality is a 'flight of the alone to the alone'. That is not a possibility for human beings. There is no human 'alone' to make such a flight. Everything human is born, fostered, transformed and expressed in the context of human community. Everything human returns to affect human community. And yet, every human individual also has a uniqueness, a particular experience, a particular perspective, a particular will and memory, a particular way of performing the common human realities, that no other human being shares in exactly the same way. In that concrete particularity, spirituality works its work.

Spirituality does not arise in the individual, however, without antecedents. While there is an irreducible individuality to each person's spirituality, that individuality is, as it were, a variation on and recombination of themes offered by the social and cultural world that shapes the individual. The variations may at times be so startling as to seem quite new. There is plenty of room for creativity, after all, in a theme and variations form. Sometimes the new variation becomes the principal theme for another generation. But one never succeeds in detaching one's individuality entirely from the social and cultural milieu. And, if one could, the results would surely prove to be entirely unintelligible to other people. Accordingly, spirituality has its communal dimensions as well as its individual ones. It takes up residence in spiritual traditions that embody and hand on a community's presuppositions about the spirituality it hopes will find a residence in its individual members. Still, the ultimate residence of spirituality is indeed in the individual, and therefore the communication of these hopes is a delicate matter, since they concern matters of the heart – something that is not open to public demonstration or inspection. Spirituality is taught more by indirection than by direct precept.

Even if spirituality resides in the individual, however, it is not a possession of the individual. Indeed, it is not a possession at all, but a relation with the unnameable Mystery to which we allude by many names. Our language is most secure in referring to the most common and observable realities. It can be fairly definite and accurate in distinguishing an elm from an oak or a chair from a stool (though a culture with only chairs and no stools or only stools and no chairs would have trouble making a distinction that comes easily to speakers of English). When it comes to things more hidden, less accessible to us, less amenable to our sustained gaze, our nouns become weaker and less exact. They become, in effect, sustained metaphors, metaphors used over and over again as if they were the literal names of things so inaccessible to us that, in fact, they cannot have names at all in the sense that one particular species, a coast live oak or an American elm, can have a name. The words are not so much efforts to identify the Mystery that is at the heart of everything as gestures meant to lead the eye of the mind to watch for that Reality, elusive but ever-present, evanescent to our perceptions but fundamental to all that is, expressible only in metaphor.

Spirituality is a relationship with this Mystery/Reality/

Truth/God. As relationship, it exists only in the way a conversation exists. If a conversation turns into a monologue on either side, it evaporates, for it can exist only in the interchange itself. So it is with spirituality. It is not merely a statement about God or to God. Nor is it merely a statement claimed to emanate from God. It exists only in so far as it is involved in exchange between the self and God. We sometimes speak of spirituality as if it were a method or a set of rules or practices: Benedictine spirituality with its Offices and its mix of prayer with manual labour, or Jesuit spirituality with its 'exercises' that seek to unite intellect and imagination in the service of discernment, or African-American spirituality with its use of music and evocation of emotion. Such methods, however, are the servants of spirituality, not its essence.

Spirituality, like conversation, is in a constant process of becoming. It is always in motion, as is appropriate to the fact that we are finite creatures. Our humanity is not fully realised or realisable in a single moment, cannot be present even to itself all at once. It is always in process of becoming. Gregory of Nyssa, accordingly, spoke of spirituality in terms of *epektasis*, a stretching out toward God rather than an arriving at God.[3] Each moment of openness to reality leaves behind it a disposition of openness to further encounter. One does not settle into a stasis, but continues moving into the infinite depths of Reality. Spirituality thus subsists neither in the human person nor in God, but in their interaction, their relationship – and specifically in the interior and consensual aspects of the relationship. For in another (and prior) sense we are all constantly in relationship with Ultimate Truth/Absolute Reality/God at all times, whether we wish to be or not, whether we are aware of it or not. We may be aware only of the daily routine, the demands of people and time and the body, putting one foot ahead of the other. But in every moment of every day, we are in fact related to every level, every aspect of reality, including the deepest ones. This external and involuntary relationship is inescapable. But it becomes spirituality or provides the foundation for spirituality when we begin to attend to it and, even to the least degree, consent to carry on a conversation with it.

I do not mean to overemphasise the consensual element in spirituality. It may be only half-conscious. It may be characterised by reluctance, anger or disbelief as easily as by eagerness or love or hope. Spirituality is not limited to those who pursue it by going on retreat or praying at fixed times or practising spiritual methods or the pieties prescribed in a particular rule of life. All these may have their utility, but the substance of spirituality is encounter with Reality at the deepest level; and that may befall the least likely person at the most improbable moment. When it happens to us, our reaction to it may be irritation, stunned disbelief, rejection, outrage or whatever; still, we are engaged, involved. Life has captured our attention in ways we can no longer escape. We cannot sink again to the level of complete unawareness. We find we have consented to participate in the conversation, even if with great reluctance and resistance. We may fight the summons. But we are engaged; we cannot merely will the experience away.

This engagement is an interior one. It resides in that aspect of human experience we often describe as the spirit or the soul. This is not to say that it leaves no traces in the exterior world. It will indeed affect every aspect of our living. The resistant Saul of Tarsus relates to God by persecuting the gospel; the converted Saul by proclaiming it. In neither case did Saul's interiority exist in isolation from external behaviour. Who we are will spill over, deliberately or not, into what we do. By insisting on the interiority of spirituality, I mean simply that spirituality is focused in an aspect of each human self to which others have no direct access. One can watch what people do, but seldom what they think or feel – and then only (if we set aside the occasional experience of clairvoyance) by the unconscious traces they leave in the person's exterior life. We are most likely to see 'through' to the interior reality when it is in motion. Like a well-camouflaged animal, it becomes invisible at rest, but we become aware of its presence when it produces change and movement.

Spirituality, precisely because of this interiority, can never be an object of direct study. As the same Paul of Tarsus put it a long time ago, 'What human being knows the things of the human being except the spirit of the human being that is in him?' (1 Corinthians 2:11). Our consciousness may not be fully accessible even to us, even from 'the inside'. It is certainly not directly accessible to others. Accordingly, one studies the spirituality of another human being through the traces it leaves in the outer world, interpreting those traces initially by analogy to one's own interior experience. Over time, one learns not to demand that others' experience be precisely like one's own; yet, there is never, I think, any other starting point when we seek to comprehend one another. As Sandra Schneiders has put it, the study of spirituality is 'self-implicating'. There is no way to pursue it without some willingness to put oneself at risk, for if I use the analogy of my own spirituality to interpret the spirituality of others, I shall eventually have to allow their spirituality to function as an analogue for my own as well. That may teach me things I didn't expect or want to learn when I began the process!

Spirituality is not accessible to the kind of 'objectivity' often assumed in other studies. This is not to say that the study of spirituality is 'subjective'. Neither term is adequate to what is actually required. Like spirituality itself, the study of spirituality involves a conversation. The student of spirituality cannot proceed without entering into the conversation in a fully personal fashion. Without introducing your own voice and experience, you will have no basis from which to work. On the other hand, you must also cultivate the ability to fall silent and listen for the voice of another. The student of spirituality is not interested in hearing merely an echo of one's own voice, a doubling of one's own experience, but rather a voice that can reveal something distinct and, for the student, new about the human conversation with God. Both the objective and the subjective must be subsumed by a mode of proceeding that we might call 'intersubjective', since it brings two or more subjects into conversation. The ensuing conversation is about the subjects' respective conversations with a reality that can be described metaphorically either as subjective ('God') or as objective ('Ultimate Reality'). There is no simple term to cover all this.

If we, at the turn of the second and third millennia, seek to study a spiritual tradition that has lived through many prior generations, we can only try to be attentive to the traces of that spirituality in the practices or writings it has created. These will offer a kind of corporeal model or reflection or byproduct of its interiority. One will look for analogy, for points of continuity with one's own experience and also for points of difference, for signs of a shared human experience and for signs of unique perspective on that experience. If the reader has in fact been extensively formed by the very writings that he now proposes to re-examine, as is the case of the present author, that will further muddy (or, to choose a more positive image, enrich) the process. And that is as it should be. Having been shaped by this poetic tradition of Anglican spirituality, I now turn back towards it in an effort to discern and record something of what distinguishes it. The process is inevitably circular, conversational, not neatly objective or subjective.

How does the poetic imagination relate to spirituality as we have been describing it? Why should lyric poetry be particularly suitable as a vehicle of spiritual discourse? What specifically in the English lyric tradition has made of it such a central and vital medium for one particular spirituality? This is a genre of writing that we usually think of as 'belonging' academically to the students of English literature, a discipline that presumes no particular interest in Christian spirituality as such. These are authors whose works can hold their own entirely as literature, allowing of course for the ebb and flow of fashion that will temporarily raise some to new prominence and sweep others away for a while. How and why did they get entangled with spirituality? Part of the reason is historical accident. Just as the Church of England began to emerge from the turmoil of Reformation and reaction in the reign of Elizabeth I, the English lyric underwent explosive development.

In some ways, the lyric is intrinsically well suited to this purpose, above all because of its erotic history. While lyric serves many purposes, one of its most ancient and enduring functions is to celebrate love; and love is intimately related and profoundly comparable to spirituality. It is comparable in that it is interior and consensual and relational. Like spirituality, it is inaccessible to direct observation. It can be observed only through the traces it leaves in the external world and communicated only by the construction of analogies that invite the reader or hearer to compare his or her own experience with that embodied in the poem. The lyric poem does not so much transcribe this interior reality as create an analogue of it for the reader, one which the reader can 'play back' by recognising the analogy and allowing it to evoke and inform and perhaps change one's own experience of the passion.

Love poetry is also typically a poetry of movement and change, for, like spirituality, love is a well-camouflaged animal, most open to detection in its movements. I think, for example, of Catullus' *Vivamus, mea Lesbia, atque amemus*:[4]

> Let's live and love, my Lesbia,
> and not count all the rumblings
> of stern old men worth a penny!
> Suns can set and rise again;
> for us, once our brief light has set,
> it's one long night of sleeping.
> Give me a thousand kisses, then a hundred,
> then another thousand, then a further hundred,
> then still another thousand, then a hundred.
> Then when we've kissed many a thousand times,
> we'll confuse the accounts. We won't even know,
> nor can some enemy cast the evil eye on us
> when he knows how many kisses we've exchanged.

First comes the piling up of kisses to incomprehensible numbers, then the suspicion that this excess may provoke the evil eye from less privileged folk. And, last, the solution: We'll tear up the accounts and start over! Somehow, in and through all this, we sense the utter absorption of lovers, their brief return to the 'surface' and rediscovery of the external world, their dismissal of it and return to their infatuation. Poetry concerned with love has always needed to express movement, change, life. It cannot remain static and achieve its goal.

A genre of poetry fashioned for the needs of love is also apt for speaking about spirituality. Not only is love, like spirituality, an interior experience that cannot be examined directly; love is relational. It is, indeed, the very substance of relation. 'Love makes the world go round.' This is not only a popular but a philosophical and theological dictum. The seventeenth-century librettist of Henry Purcell's *The Fairy Queen* plays on it ironically in a song in which Phoebus (the Sun) boasts that Love is dependent on him while at the same time acknowledging that all things depend on Love:

> 'Tis I who give life, warmth and vigour to all;
> Even Love who rules all things in earth, air and sea
> Would languish and fade, and to nothing would fall;
> The world to its chaos would return but for me.

Yet, the Sun is not the true source of any of this exuberance, but Eros. Love is not only analogous to spirituality, it is of the substance of it, as spiritual teachers have long insisted. The delicate problem of speaking about an interior relationship with Ultimate Reality/Absolute Truth/God can thus be resolved (in so far as it ever can be) by taking up a set of tools devised to express human love, which is not only analogous to the divine love, but in some sense continuous with it. This, of course, was no new idea in the Renaissance, since Christians had been reading the Song of Songs in this fashion from early in their history.[5]

Yet another element of lyric poetry that lent itself to the use of spiritual discourse was its ability to embody fleeting and elusive elements of experience in the form of concrete models. In this respect, lyric poetry is very nearly the opposite genre to theological or philosophical writing. Where theological or philosophical writing abstracts and generalises, lyric tends to

concretise, to build a small world in which the hidden forces at
work in the great world become tangible and observable for
a moment. Take, for example, Robert Herrick's 'Upon Julia's
Clothes':

> Whenas in silks my Julia goes
> Then, then, methinks, how sweetly flows
> That liquefaction of her clothes.
>
> Next, when I cast mine eyes and see
> That brave vibration each way free,
> O how that glittering taketh me![6]

The external image of Julia in her silk dress becomes an image
of the internal erotic forces that 'melt' the speaker of the poem
and compel devoted attention. The whole poem reconstitutes a
brief moment of sight and the way such a sight can both give
rise to and embody a world of feeling. Where expository prose
might endeavour to abstract some timeless principle of the
erotic, lyric poetry aims to achieve such timelessness, if at all,
only through the medium of its embodiment in a particular
moment.

Nonetheless, lyric remains a mode of communication, seeking
to give some words to our interiority that might allow it to
emerge and become part of a discourse shared among human
beings. Some readers, to be sure, may object to the notion of
poetry as communication, preferring to treat it as a kind
of abstract art with words as its medium. I doubt, however,
whether the art of word placement has alone constituted the
primary appeal of poetry, even for the most cultivated reader.
The power of lyric lies not only in its power to order language in
musical ways, powerful as that is, but in its ability to bring us
face to face with experience – often our own experience in a form
we had not yet recognised, sometimes experience that, while
remaining alien to us in some significant way, still casts a new
light on our own. By this I mean not that the lyric poem
embodies the experience of the reader as such but that the
reader reads the lyric by the analogy of one's own experience,

the reader's experience overlapping that incarnated in the poem by the poet. What one meets, in this process, is partly the experience thus concretised by the poet and partly the experience of the reader thrown, in this way, into sharper relief by light from a new angle.

Admittedly, the unreflective notion that a poet simply records her or his own experience cannot account for what we actually find in lyric. Lyric poems are not simple transcriptions of their authors' experience, though that may at times be a significant element in their composition. The 'I' of the poem is not always the 'I' of the author's own life. Yet lyric poetry of genuine life and energy emerges not from indifference but from engagement. If the poet is not engaged with life, the poetry is flat. If the poet's involvement takes the second-hand, shopworn form of sentimentality, the poetry is banal. If the poet does not succeed in connecting the written word with experience (both the poet's and the reader's), no amount of skill will produce a work that captures the reader.

A lyric poem, then, is not a transcript of the author's experience that can be held up next to that of the reader and compared with it. Rather the poem is a little world built to convey something of the larger world, something rooted in experience. In any case, it would be impossible to transcribe experience without interpreting it in the process – nor to read a poem without further interpreting it in that process. The relationship of poetry to the poet's unique, immediate experience will normally remain less than perfectly clear. Its rooting in human experience is what continues central for us. The point of a love poem is not that it leads us to speculate on the author's sex life; the point is that it enables us to have a language for the hidden force of love as experienced by human beings.

In sixteenth- and seventeenth-century England, lyric poetry was, of course, only one mode of communication among the many available. The importance of its role in Anglican spirituality can be recognised only by setting it alongside other significant modes. One of these was the spiritual treatise, such as Jeremy Taylor's *Rule and Exercises of Holy Living*, which tended to take a prescriptive approach to matters of spirituality. Another was moral theology, another personal counsel.[7] Yet another was the sermon, which, at the time, was often close to the lyric poem in its use of rhetorical device and vivid imagery.[8] Still, the sermon also was inclined to prescribe to its listeners and to define belief for them. The same was true for theological treatises. The liturgical language of common prayer, while often richly poetic, was addressed primarily to God and presented a portrait of the speakers (the congregation) that conformed to general types more than to individual experience. The lyric poem, by contrast, presented an analogue of personal experience that could be 'overheard' without its directly prescribing belief or behaviour. It offered rather a point of comparison and perhaps illumination. It created an opportunity to discourse about the hidden, interior realities of spirituality. Lyric has never been the sole genre of Anglican spirituality, but it has offered a particular opportunity which the poets were quick to accept.

One particular factor encouraging this development was the contemporary prominence of the sonnet as a genre, particularly in its 'English' form, in which a final couplet breaks the patterns established in the preceding three quatrains. The sonnet is a form built pre-eminently on contrast, on relationship and opposition, movement and change. It has about it a certain formal impetus encouraging an alteration of perspective, a moment of discovery. In this way, it was already adapted to the needs of spiritual discourse. Given the relational and living nature of spirituality, as we have said, it will be most readily and authentically perceived in motion. The sonnet reveals much because it expects alteration and development. While the sonnet was by no means the exclusive form for lyric in the period, even those poets who wrote in other forms often borrowed the sonnet's tendency to make a sharp turn toward the end. For that matter, this turn has its roots much further back, specifically in love poetry, as exemplified in the poem of Catullus quoted above.

One other contemporary literary form seems to have offered

possibilities similar to those of the lyric poem – the short prose meditation as found in Donne's *Devotions upon Emergent Occasions* or Traherne's *Centuries of Meditations*. In this genre, there is more of a prose element, an element of commentary on experience and even interpretation of it in theological or philosophical terms. Still, experience itself remains central, and the interpretation is frequently offered in the analogical mode found also in lyric poetry, by constructing a little world in which the reader can find overlapping experience. Accordingly, the meditation can sometimes share lyric poetry's ability to form a bridge between the interior experience of one person and another.

Such bridges are welcome not because they absorb our attention entirely as readers, but because they also direct our attention outward (or perhaps, in this case, I should say 'inward') to some aspect of our reality that we find illumined by them. In this, they perform a function like that of scripture as described by Wilfred Cantwell Smith:

> [Traditional reading of scripture] aimed at proffering not, in the fashion of modern exegesis, 'the meaning of the text', but the meaning of the universe, of world history, of human life: of the readers' own lives as they read, or as they set forth about their affairs after reading. They aspired to that meaning considered in the light of the words here proffered. Considered in the light of 'the text', one might say, except that on reflection it becomes clear that this too will not do; we shall be arguing that the idea of a text, as an object to be understood, is modern and impersonal and subordinating, characterizing present-day culture's objectivizing orientation to the world. Their intent was rather to discern that meaning in the light of what God had to say to them.[9]

There is always a larger reality on which the worshipper expects to find the scriptures casting light. Lyric poetry is read for just such reasons, even by those for whom this notion of a 'larger reality' has no conventionally religious overtones.

In these ways, lyric poetry, particularly as it existed in the sixteenth and seventeenth centuries, lent itself extremely well to the uses of emergent Reformation Anglican spirituality. It was capable of taking inner experience, externalising and concretising it in the form of a little poetic world that the reader/hearer could then relate analogically to her internal experience, and of doing this in a way that allowed for movement, for a shift, a turn, a transformation. One might even say, using the language of Christian spirituality, 'a conversion'. Conversion, in this case, means not the transition from one religion to another, but rather the kind of spiritual awakening and revolution that the New Testament authors embody in the Greek term *metanoia*. Another name for it might be 'discovery of grace'. As we shall see, this was a particularly important element in the spirituality that the Anglican poets embodied in their lyrics.[10]

ENGLISH AND ANGLICAN: THE CONTEXT OF THE TRADITION

To this point, we have dealt in relatively general terms with the relation between spirituality and lyric poetry. Now we turn our attention to the specifically Anglican context for their interaction. And this raises the question of what one means by the word 'Anglican'. In one sense, it is an easy question to answer. The Anglican Communion is a kind of 'family' of churches whose ancestry is rooted in the shape that English-speaking Christianity took on in the Church of England at the Reformation. This is not to deny the importance of older elements, such as patristic theology and medieval English mysticism, that continued to shape post-Reformation Anglicanism, nor of later reinterpretations of Anglican life and thought such as the Evangelical, Oxford and Liturgical Movements, nor of the sweeping contemporary change implied by the accelerating expansion of the Anglican churches of the Third World. It is only to repeat the commonplace that Anglicanism is a form of catholic Christianity that went through a more sweeping reformation than did the Church of Rome but still remained and remains less purely protestant than the churches more directly involved in or influenced by the continental Reformation. Anglicanism is a fact on the ground of modern Christianity, identified both by this shared history and by an ongoing sense of familial connection, with the Archbishop of Canterbury as senior cousin. It is relatively clear *who* is Anglican: anyone who claims the history and is claimed by the family.

That said, it is less clear *what* is Anglican. What makes an idea or a tradition or a spirituality 'Anglican'? I never understood how difficult it is to answer such questions until I began serving on ecumenical dialogues between Lutherans and Anglicans and found myself trying to explicate Anglicanism for people whose presuppositions about how an ecclesiastical tradition originates and understands itself were radically different. Lutherans wanted to know where our confessions were, what were our core doctrines, how we established doctrinal norms. We tended to point to liturgy as the focus of our tradition. But even in liturgy, we have only limited consensus. Worldwide, the Anglican Communion embraces everything from forms of catholicism that make the post-Vatican II Roman liturgy look decidedly protestant to forms of charismatic and evangelical church life that make most American Presbyterians look liturgically very high church. How does one describe what unites these disparate practices, however precariously, in one communion?

Anglicanism, though it is a real enough phenomenon, is an elusive notion. One knows it when one sees it, not just in its characteristic middle-of-the-road manifestation, but at its most catholic and its most protestant, at its most insular and its most global, at its best and most likeable or its worst and most tiresome. But how to define or even to describe it? Although Anglicans have elements that distinguish our tradition from those of, say, Lutherans or Roman Catholics, we have nothing at all that is entirely distinctive to us. Do we have bishops? So do most Christians. Do we have a traditional liturgy? So do most Christians. The fact of our liturgy being in the vernacular once set us apart from other catholics, but it does so no longer. Do we say the ancient creeds? Yes, and so do most other Christians.

There seems to be nothing at all that is uniquely Anglican. Yet this does not mean that Anglicanism is colourless, that it disappears when held up against other traditions as a background. As a friend once said to me, 'Anglicanism, as a form of Christianity, has nothing distinctive about it, except the fact that it has nothing distinctive about it, which is, of course, very distinctive indeed.'[11] But there is more than that.

Truth to tell, it is not sufficient to say that Anglicanism eludes definition. It would be more accurate to say that it positively resists it. And this is more than a convenient metaphor. It seems to have been an animating principle as far back as the Reformation, when it became important for Western Christian communities to distinguish themselves doctrinally from one another. In the sixteenth and seventeenth centuries, Anglicanism declined to commit its energies to the writing of confessions in the currently fashionable mode. The Thirty-nine Articles are, at best, a poor relation of their Lutheran and Reformed kin or of the detailed definitions of the Council of Trent.[12] They are perhaps the least prepossessing document one could have at the time and still claim to have some principles. If the early Oxford Movement in the nineteenth century found them open to almost infinite reinterpretation, that is at least partly because they were framed to say so little in the first place.[13]

Reformation Anglicanism did, of course, have its polemical writers. Yet they seem to have had only a secondary effect in determining the nature of Anglicanism. There is no Anglican Bellarmine. Anglicanism did not have either a unique principle like papal primacy in the Roman Church or a highly coherent, systematic doctrine like that which came to characterise Reformed Christianity. Without these, it was in a weak position to assert its own doctrinal supremacy. Instead, it found its most helpful interpreters (notably Richard Hooker) in its apologists – those who defended it against the attacks of Christians who 'knew' more.[14] It might be useful to think of Reformation Anglicanism as having defined itself against what it saw as the *over-*

definition of others. Hence the difficulty ever after in giving it, or discerning in it, sharp outlines.

The word 'Anglicanism' is of nineteenth-century origin. The bare form of the word implies an intellectually coherent, clearly bounded phenomenon on a par with Lutheranism, Presbyterianism, Methodism, Roman Catholicism. It suggests at least a predictable stance in relation to Christian faith if not an out-and-out systematic theology. Accordingly, it misleads. While Anglicanism was shaped or reshaped quite emphatically in the Reformation, its experience also differed significantly from the other churches that passed through that furnace and from more recent traditions such as Methodism or Pentecostalism that have arisen in their image. The great difference is that the others have at their root an idea, while Anglicanism has at its root a *community* and a *conversation*. Reformation Anglicanism was not so much an idea in search of a community, as a community in search of a revised self-understanding. The ultimate product was like all decisions of families under stress. It may well not have been any one person's preferred solution; it emerged in a dialogue of diverse principles with one another and with the practical possibilities of community life. It was not the creation of a hierarchy or of a solitary religious or theological genius, but of a complex compromise between monarch, peers, people and church leaders.[15]

What defines Anglicanism as a communion today? On any appraisal, we are short of clear boundary markers. Eventually, in explaining ourselves to others, we have to turn to history or genealogy rather than to a top-down kind of theological deduction. Since the Church of England, both before and after the Reformation, was the 'unmarked' form of English Christianity, it required no further definition.[16] It was the recusants on the one hand and the dissenters on the other who had to define themselves and who show a corresponding preoccupation, in their writings, with distinctive doctrines.[17] Anglicanism was, as it were, the family religion. In the difficult times of the Tudor era and the Reformation, when the political stakes were tremendously high, the family religion bumbled its way through to some sort of solution. It is difficult to speak highly of bumbling. But, then again, there may be situations so unclear that bumbling is the highest form of wisdom and the one most likely to produce life-giving results.

Anglicanism rejected the refurbishing of medieval Western catholicism by Trent. But it also rejected a more precisely prot- estant self-definition as offered by the more extreme Puritans. This twin refusal became a constitutional preference. Angli- canism is an extremely traditional form of Christianity, favouring the doctrinal formulations of the third and fourth centuries over those of later ages and clinging to sometimes archaic forms of worship. Yet, it has remained suspicious of thoroughgoing systematic presentations of Christianity, including conservative ones. Indeed, it has remained suspicious of all conceptions of Christianity that know too much, whether through the hubris of the intellect or the unwary pride of 'enthusiasm'. (The Methodists of the eighteenth century seemed as dangerous in their own way as the Puritans and Romans of the seventeenth.) We are more the children of the sixteenth- century Humanists with their broad interest in all forms of human knowledge and experience than of the Scholastics, cath- olic or protestant, with their intellectual ambitions, or of such powerful individuals as Luther or John Wesley with their inten- sity of feeling and purpose. We are doubtful that detailed definition makes God more accessible or that intense feeling can command the Spirit. We are, in a word, defined largely by a sometimes inarticulate refusal of definition.

This leaves us to say that we are a communion, a family. A recent spokesman has suggested that the Anglican communion is defined by who gets invited to what meetings by the Arch- bishop of Canterbury.[18] Even allowing for the danger of bureaucratic trivialisation implicit in that definition, it grasps the essentially relational element in Anglicanism. It is not defined primarily by doctrine, though it is doctrinally and lit- urgically traditional. It is defined in terms of a continuum of people in relationship to one another and to God, a kind of family. Even our traditionalism is simply the extension of this relational principle to our co-believers of past and future.

As relationship, Anglicanism can be gestured toward, alluded to, sometimes even described, but scarcely defined. This evanescence in Anglican reality was perhaps reinforced by the characteristic Platonism of post-Reformation Anglican theologians. Truth, for Anglicans, tends to be seen, often quite unconsciously, in terms of Platonic *idea* – something that can be approached, but not possessed within the confines of the phenomenal world. One may move toward it in this age, but never stand directly in its full presence – certainly not command that presence or grasp it. At most, one can be grasped by it, which means, for those so grasped, an ongoing process of transformation. From this proceeds a pervasive Anglican scepticism about claims of doctrinal or moral perfection. Some Anglicans, of course, have claimed a certain degree of perfection for Anglicanism itself; there is an Anglican triumphalism to match that of Roman Catholics or Lutherans. But Anglicans in general have been reluctant to invest much energy in such claims.

One may note that there are certain parallels between Anglicanism thus described and what I have said earlier about spirituality. I emphatically do not wish to identify the two with each other, but the overlaps may have focused some particular characteristics of Anglican spirituality. In both cases, relationship is the predominant category, not the apparent objectivity of ideas. Neither is reducible to system. Neither can exist in a single representative or representation. Neither God nor the human being can one-sidedly determine spirituality. Similarly, no single expression of Anglicanism, whether in the form of a book, a confession, a parish, a diocese, an ecclesiastical party, a theology, can ever settle what Anglicanism is. It is all these things and more in an ongoing conversation with one another.

All this is frequently seasoned with a strong dash of scepticism or outright agnosticism. Most Anglicans do not seem to support the outright rejection of traditional Christian doctrine by figures like James A. Pike. But they are also inclined to be suspicious of those who would flatten out the metaphorical character of religious and spiritual discourse and speak of theology as if it had the same clear, closed and definitive character as a shopping list. It is characteristic of Anglicanism to insist on the 'real presence' of Christ in the Eucharist while rejecting the conventional late medieval explanation of that presence in the doctrine of transubstantiation. One must not pretend to know too much.

In the following pages, I will offer a survey of the poetic expression of Anglican spirituality in English lyric poetry. I will draw my illustrations almost entirely from British poets of major reputation in the canon of English literature, the one exception being the contemporary Australian poet Judith Wright. I have also limited my comments for the most part to poets whose works and lives show a strong Anglican connection. As will become clear in the following pages, the thematic patterns I am tracing have long ago ceased to be unique to Anglican writers. Yet, they are rooted there. Nor are they to be found only in the major figures of the literary canon. Yet, it is through their writings that most of us are first exposed to this spirituality. And through their work, what begins as a specifically Anglican response to the work of God's Spirit has become a fixture of English-language literary culture.

The very fact that this spirituality has embodied itself in poetry rather than in prose has consequences for the tradition. It encourages it to stay close to the experiential and to share itself in a conversation of equals rather than move toward issuing rules and directions and taking shape as a school in which those who know everything instruct those who know nothing. It has much to say, then, both about what Anglican spirituality can offer the reader and about what it cannot – and would not wish to – give.

2. RESOURCES OF IMAGE AND LANGUAGE

Looking for the spirituality incarnate in English lyric poetry, we may assume that we are concerned primarily with its content; but, in poetry, one can never entirely disentangle the content of the work from the medium – the poetic tradition of language created, shared, imitated, rejected, revised and re-created over centuries. Part of what distinguishes the Anglican poetic tradition is its stock of language and metaphor, marked by certain features that reappear repeatedly, though not in every poet's work. These are the raw (or, to be more exact, partially refined) materials from which the poet constructs the poem that can serve as an analogue of spiritual experience. They form the shared medium of communication, accessible to both writer and reader, that makes the sharing of such experience possible. Without this medium, we have no access to what lies in and under it. The Anglican poetic tradition has certain characteristic elements, including a high (but distinctive) regard for scripture, a sense of the spiritual value of nature, an investment in the life of the church, and a sense of the accessibility of the Holy in and through the ordinary and the childlike. Each calls for some treatment here.

SCRIPTURE AND THE RELIGIOUS SPHERE

The peculiar place of *scripture* owes much to the way in which the English Reformers made the reading of it a central activity of faith and created a specifically Anglican context for it in the Daily Office,[1] which placed the reading of scripture in the primary context of common prayer rather than that of theological reflection or polemic. Not that the intellectual approach to scripture was absent, but that it took second place; the first thing one did with scripture was to read it in the context of public worship. Where theological reading of scripture has traditionally sought to answer questions of doctrine and morals, the context of prayer orients the reading of scripture to human needs and hopes and to the spiritual intimacy of which prayer is a religious model and expression.[2] In the study, one wants ideas from scripture. In the church one wants something that can be prayed or sung. Hence scripture is often used by Anglicans, especially the earlier poets, not only as a source of ideas but also as a shared language full of rich and productive images.[3] There is a certain intimacy with scripture in this poetry, prompted by the worshippers' having heard it, over and over, in the liturgical context of prayer and praise. It becomes a language for conversation with God.

For example, George Herbert's poem 'Discipline' depends on the reader's making several important connections with scriptural language. It begins by summoning up (and protesting) a picture of a wrathful punishing God:

> Throw away thy rod,
> Throw away thy wrath:
> Oh my God,
> Take the gentle path.

The image of God's punishing wrath is so widespread in scripture as not to require being tied to any particular verse; but the biblical references become more specific as the poem moves forward. The speaker wants God to exchange wrath for love:

> Then let wrath remove;
> Love will do the deed:
> For with love
> Stony hearts will bleed. (lines 17–20)

Here, the reader may well be reminded of Paul's paean to love: '[charity] beareth all things, believeth all things, hopeth all things, endureth all things. Charity never faileth.' There is also an allusion to the divine promise that 'I will put a new spirit within you; and I will take the stony heart out of their flesh, and will give them an heart of flesh'.[4]

The speaker continues:

> Love is swift of foot;
> Love's a man of war,
>   And can shoot,
> And can hit from far. (lines 21–4)[5]

Here, 'swift of foot' is a Hebraism, maintaining the biblical quality of the language, though no particular verse seems to be evoked. The next phrase ('Love's a man of war'), however, has a quite specific source. It alludes to the song of Moses: 'The LORD is my strength and song, and he is become my salvation: he is my God, and I will prepare him an habitation; my father's God, and I will exalt him. The LORD is a man of war, the LORD is his name.'[6] The statement 'Love's a man of war' will resonate in the mind of the person familiar with scripture as 'God is a man of war'. By creating this resonance, Herbert has subtly evoked yet another biblical passage: 'God is love.'[7]

This sort of allusive, playful use of scripture pervades the tradition. There are poets who make little or no use of it; and it has perhaps become less useful and less usable in the twentieth century, with the decline of biblical literacy. But it has never disappeared. Judith Wright's 'In Praise of Marriages' begins:

> Not till life halved, and parted
> one from the other,
> did time begin, and knowledge;
> sorrow, delight. (lines 1–4)[8]

The 'halving' of life can be read in several ways – as a reference to the evolution of sexual difference, to the process of mitosis that produces egg and sperm, as a reference to birth, as an allusion to the myth of the original two-headed human being in Plato's *Symposium*. But it also implies some reference to Genesis 2—3, the dividing of Eve from Adam and the subsequent story of the Fall, which involved eating the fruit of the 'tree of knowledge of good and evil'. After the Fall, 'Adam knew his wife' – a Hebrew euphemism for sexual intercourse. While the poem is intelligible without the reader's recognising the scriptural dimensions of its language, it loses much of its richness.

This allusive use of scripture in English lyric poetry is a product of the fact that the Bible was, until relatively recently, a shared cultural possession of English-speaking people. Henry Vaughan could address the Bible thus:

> Thou wert the first put in my hand,
> When yet I could not understand,
> And daily didst my young eyes lead
> To letters, till I learned to read.
>
> ('To the Holy Bible', lines 5–8)[9]

For Anglicans, however, there is also, lying behind this fact, a particular manner of approaching the Bible that grants this allusive use of scripture its spiritual authority. As already mentioned, Anglicans have emphasised the reading of scripture in the context of prayer. Like other churches of the Reformation, Anglicans also made use of scripture as a theological pruning hook to trim the luxuriance of late medieval Western catholicism.[10] Anglicans did not, however, join with the more extreme Reformed (in England, the Puritans) in the pursuit of a completely biblical system of religion. Those Puritans who could remain conscientiously within the Church of England were not actively hindered until the time of Charles I; but the larger church refused to commit itself to their position. What developed, then, among Anglicans was a different way of thinking about scripture – a vision of scripture not so much as a kind of divine law, containing detailed blueprints for the Christian religion, but rather as a promise, a gospel, even perhaps a letter from a dear friend. The Bible was looked to for the assurance of grace more than for the details of church life and belief.[11]

George Herbert, in the poem 'Discipline' cited above, replaces the angry image of God that was vital to more extreme versions of the Calvinist doctrine of double predestination with the image of God as love. In doing so, he writes, as we have seen, in a language dense with biblical allusion. More than that, he makes his appeal to the Bible explicit:

> Not a word or look
> I affect to own,
>   But by book,
> And thy book alone. (lines 9–12)[12]

While one can read this stanza simply as validation of the speaker's appeal to God, it also counters certain other claims about the Bible, claims suggesting that its principal purport was to expound God's righteous anger toward the human race, an anger that would justify the condemnation of the great mass of humanity to hell.

Henry Vaughan's references to scripture reveal a similar tension with the Reformed. He describes the Bible as working on him not through fear but through kindness:

> By this mild art of love at length
> Thou overcam'st my sinful strength,
> And having brought me home, didst there
> Show me that pearl I sought elsewhere.
> Gladness, and peace, and hope, and love,
> The secret favours of the Dove,
> Her quickening kindness, smiles and kisses,
> Exalted pleasures, crowning blisses,
> Fruition, union, glory, life
> Thou didst lead to, and still all strife.
>   ('To the Holy Bible', lines 23–32)[13]

In itself, this celebration of the Bible's influence may not seem distinctive, but it stands in strong contrast to the extreme Calvinist emphasis on the desperate sinfulness of humanity – something Vaughan attacks in his poem 'The Agreement'.[14] Here, the speaker reclaims the scriptures as source of hope, after others have misled him into seeing in them only condemnation. He addresses the Bible:

> O beamy book! O my mid-day
> Exterminating fears and night!
>   . . .
>> Each page of thine hath true life in't,
>> And God's bright mind expressed in print.
>>   (lines 13–14, 23–4)

By contrast with the Bible:

> Most modern books are blots on thee,
> Their doctrine chaff and windy fits:
> Darkened along, as their scribes be,
> With those foul storms, when they were writ;
>> While thee man's zeal lays out, and blends
>> Only self-worship and self-ends.
>   . . .
> For until thou didst comfort me,
> I had not one poor word to say;
> Thick busy clouds did multiply,
> And said, I was no child of day;
>> They said, my own hands did remove
>> That candle given me from above. (lines 25–30, 37–42)

Only reading the Bible for the hope of grace can deliver the poet from the despair inflicted by those who read it particularly for a doctrine of damnation.

In a similar vein, Thomas Traherne wrote of 'The Bible':

>> That! That! There I was told
>> That I the son of God was made,
>> His image. O divine! (lines 1–3)[15]

The surprising, ecstatic discovery of relatedness to God, made tangible by the almost inarticulate double exclamation with which the poem begins – this is the essential heart of the Bible. It is a message leading toward conversion and new hope, not a pronouncement of condemnation and a series of prescriptions for belief and behaviour.

This approach to scripture leaves the poet free to wrestle with the text of scripture in ways that might strike the outsider as irreverent, as R. S. Thomas does in his address to Paul. He corrects the apostle for asking 'Who art thou, Lord?' during his experience on the Damascus Road:

> Wrong question, Paul. Who am I,
> Lord? is what you should have asked.
> And the answer, surely, somebody
> who it is easy for us to kick against.[16]

Distinctively modern as this questioning may seem, it is implicit in the work of the seventeenth-century poets – in Herbert's use of scripture to give love priority over an equally scriptural wrath, or in Vaughan's appeal to scripture itself as message of grace against those who claimed to be its authentic interpreters.

However deeply Anglicans revere scripture, we have tended to retain an awareness of the human element in it.[17] It is the Word of God, but that does not necessarily mean that it is God's words. Always, the Bible is second to the incarnate Word. Scripture contains the sure word of promise, the word of gracious release – but not without an admixture of human misunderstanding. W. H. Auden captures the tradition's odd blend of scepticism and hope in relation to scripture in a passage from his Christmas oratorio *For the Time Being*:

> Though written by Thy children with
>   A smudged and crooked line,
> Thy Word is ever legible,
> Thy Meaning unequivocal,
> And for Thy Goodness even sin
>   Is valid as a sign.
>
> Inflict Thy promises with each
>   Occasion of distress,
> That from our incoherence we
> May learn to put our trust in Thee,
> And brutal fact persuade us to
>   Adventure, Art, and Peace.

('Chorale', lines 7–18)[18]

As we have said, scripture, among Anglicans, is largely mediated through liturgy. Even though it is also studied outside the context of the church service, the context of worship particularly determines how it has meaning. Echoes of scripture, then, as echoes of the service, tend to function as prayer. Much of the other language and imagery with which our poets speak about spirituality also emerges from *the worship of the church*. Religion is not, of course, identical with spirituality. It may even act as a defence against spirituality. One can be quite meticulously and energetically religious without letting it touch one's inner life in any telling way. But religion is the way cultures convey their assumptions about God and self and world and offer a context for experiencing and interpreting our relationship with Ultimate Truth. Religion is a model constructed on the basis of our spiritual experience, but once it is called into existence, it is also a formative influence on that experience. It provides the expectations with which we go to our meeting with God, the language in which we try to speak of the meeting – and sometimes even the context in which the meeting takes place.[19]

It is a truism that the religious practice of Anglicanism, ever since the Reformation, has been centred primarily on common prayer. Anglicanism has dealt with most of its major conflicts liturgically. They take on liturgical form and they are resolved, if at all, by liturgical means. In the American Revolution, for example, Patriot Anglicans and Tory Anglicans defined themselves by their choice of which government to pray for. After the war, the new American Episcopal Church defined itself by revising its Book of Common Prayer. Worldwide, Anglicanism has defined itself as a 'communion', a body of people united by receiving (or at least by being willing to receive) communion with one another. We worship together and so know one another as sisters and brothers. When our internal fights reach dangerous levels, we threaten to quit worshipping together. When we revise our liturgical forms, the process occasions strains and anxieties that, in other denominations, would be more likely to attend conflicts over matters of doctrine or morals.

This does not, paradoxically, mean that public worship is the main concern of Anglicans. It is, under most circumstances, our medium, not our message. Medium and message, to be sure, are intimately linked and easily confused. They restrict and shape each other mutually. But they are not identical. This is no doubt the reason why our poets spend very little time celebrating or even speaking of liturgy as such. George Herbert's work may seem at first to be an exception. His collection of spiritual poetry is called *The Temple* and it makes many references to portions of the church building, elements of the liturgy, and moments in the Christian year. There are poems called 'The Church Porch', 'The Altar' (a poem that actually forms an image of that piece of ecclesiastical furniture), 'Church Monuments', 'Holy Baptism', 'Holy Communion', 'Easter Wings', 'Whit-Sunday' and so forth.

Liturgy pervades these poems less as their topic than as an assumption, a given of religious experience that can therefore provide a language in which the poet moves toward the experience of the spirit. Herbert rejoices in the common prayer of the church as a place of sacraments and penitence and praise, all the things that signify our approach to God, but he does not, finally, give common prayer the central place. It is a means to an end – an end in which the means participates, but which it does not achieve by itself. In 'Antiphon (I)', he summons 'all the world' to sing 'My God and King':

> The heav'ns are not too high,
> His praise may thither fly:
> The earth is not too low,
> His praises there may grow. (lines 3–6)

And he summons the church, too. It must do its praising in the proper Anglican way, with the psalms that form so large an element in Morning and Evening Prayer:

> The church with psalms must shout,
> No door can keep them out: (lines 9–10)

The joy of praising God, however, finds its ultimate home not in the public worship of the church but in the soul communing with the Holy:

> But above all, the heart
> Must bear the longest part. (lines 11–12)[20]

Other poets, too, celebrate and make use of the liturgy. Vaughan, for example, emphasises the shared community of prayer. But the service in itself does not guarantee anything. He finds, in fact, that only the intervention of God's grace makes participation in prayer possible:

> O how in this thy choir of souls I stand
> > (Propped by thy hand)
> > A heap of sand!
> Which busy thoughts (like winds) would scatter quite
> > And put to flight,
> > But for thy might;
> > Thy hand alone doth tame
> > Those blasts, and knit my frame,
> > > ('Church-Service', lines 9–16)[21]

John Betjeman even celebrates this wandering of the attention as a kind of prayer in its own right. The straying path of the mind, taking its departure from the service, may offer at times, in indirect and unlikely ways, a moment of access to the Divine. In 'Sunday Afternoon Service in St Enodoc Church, Cornwall', the clergyman begins the service:

> . . . and a bumble-bee
> Zooms itself free into the churchyard sun
> And so my thought this happy Sabbathtide.
> > Where deep cliffs loom enormous, where cascade
> Mesembryanthemum and stone-crop down,
> Where the gull looks no larger than a lark
> Hung midway twixt the cliff-top and the sand
> Sun-shadowed valleys roll along the sea.

The speaker's meditation rambles across the dashing of the

waves and the solidity of the slate that undergirds the region
and so back to the church built of it and the obscure St Enodoc
to whom it owes its name, the whole culminating in an awareness of death that returns him to the words of the service itself:

> What faith was his, that dim, that Cornish saint,
> Small rushlight of a long-forgotten church,
> Who lived with God on this unfriendly shore,
> Who knew He made the Atlantic and the stones
> And destined seamen here to end their lives
> Dashed on a rock, rolled over in the surf,
> And not one hair forgotten. Now they lie
> In centuries of sand beside the church.
> Less pitiable are they than the corpse
> Of a large golfer, only four weeks dead,
> This sunlit and sea-distant afternoon.
> 'Praise ye the Lord!' and in another key
> The Lord's name by harmonium be praised.
> 'The Second Evening and the Fourteenth Psalm.'
>
> (lines 79–86, 107–20)[22]

W. H. Auden sometimes speaks of the way in which the round
of the Christian year may confront us with spiritual realities we
might otherwise avoid acknowledging in our world. Ascension
Day is

> This Thursday when we must
> Go through the ritual
> Formulae of farewell.
>
> ('Ascension Day, 1964', lines 28–30)[23]

But the central thing is not liturgy as such, but rather the way
liturgy (often in tandem with scripture) creates a language of
word and image that the poet makes use of to draw the reader
toward truths that lie too deep for ordinary speech. Thus
Christina Rossetti, in 'Goblin Market', draws upon the language
of the Eucharist to reveal the union of flesh and spirit involved
in one person's sacrifice to give life to another. One sister, Laura,
has tasted the goblin fruits and is now dying of despair because

they are no more to be had. The other sister, Lizzie, who (unlike Laura) can still hear the goblins crying their wares, visits them and, with great ingenuity and at savage cost to herself, provokes them to smash their fruits against her mouth in a vain effort to get her, too, to taste of them. On returning, her face still wet with the juices,

> She cried, 'Laura,' up the garden,
> 'Did you miss me?
> Come and kiss me.
> Never mind my bruises,
> Hug me, kiss me, suck my juices
> Squeezed from goblin fruits for you,
> Goblin pulp and goblin dew.
> Eat me, drink me, love me;
> Laura, make much of me:
> For your sake I have braved the glen
> And had to do with goblin merchant men.'
>
> (lines 464–74)[24]

The poem's juxtaposition of a fairy-tale environment and a fleshly and erotic richness of language and imagery with the words of the Eucharist is shocking, but not in a chance way or merely for the sake of shock. Rossetti is unveiling, with the help of liturgical language and experience, the saving possibilities of human love. As in eating the body of Christ and drinking his blood, the worshipper receives the communion of God's love, so in the sacrifice of one person to give another life a new communion of persons is created.

'THE WORLD'

Religion, however pervasive its influence in the Anglican poetic tradition, has by no means been the only element that shaped it. Anglicanism, on the whole, seems to avoid the more extreme Reformed tendency to identify the 'world' as the 'enemy'. On the contrary, the daily recitation of belief in a God who is 'maker of heaven and earth' has had its effect. While Anglicans have not always placed encounter with God outside the confines of Christian religion on the same plane with the Bible or common prayer, we have assumed that the same God is indeed operative both within the church and beyond it. In ordinary parlance, 'the world' is often deliberately contrasted with 'the church' as the realm of the secular, the unhallowed, the non-religious. For the secularist, the 'world' is the realm where religion is at last unveiled as irrelevant and useless; for the pietist, it is the realm where salvation is impossible and the soul will surely be lost. Anglicanism as a whole has not consented to this sharp dualism of church and world. And, having left the door to the world ajar, it finds that the world has a good deal to say to the life of the spirit. Indeed, the life of the spirit goes on largely in the context of the world, not in the narrowly religious segment of our lives.

The 'world' manifests itself in a variety of ways in the tradition of Anglican poetry, but a particularly important mode is that of *nature*. 'Nature' here does not always mean what the twentieth-century reader would mean by it. The earlier poets, in particular, often moralise it or allegorise it, giving it specifically religious meanings. Yet, there is no mistaking their fascination with the natural world in its own right, a fascination that inspires not merely use of natural imagery but delight in the natural world as a way toward God.

George Herbert's second poem entitled 'Easter' is a good example. The panoply of nature is evoked to set apart a day of the church calendar. These are not shy, retiring metaphors; nature forces itself upon our senses here. The poem virtually recreates the sights and smells for us:

> I got me flowers to straw thy way;
> I got me boughs off many a tree:
> But thou wast up by break of day,
> And brought'st thy sweets along with thee.
>
> The Sun arising in the East,
> Though he give light, and th'East perfume;

> If they should offer to contest
> With thy arising, they presume.
>
> Can there be any day but this,
> Though many suns to shine endeavour?
> We count three hundred, but we miss:
> There is but one, and that one ever.[25]

In one sense, the Easter of nature, of the trees and the sun, is being set aside to be replaced by the eternal Easter. Yet, it is only by the vividness of nature's Easter that one gains any sense of the riches of the eternal one. Nature here becomes as good a language for spirituality as scripture. This is not 'natural theology,' to be sure. It is not theology at all in the intellectual sense. It is a matter of seizing upon everything in human experience that may reveal the possibilities of our human intimacy with God.

Henry Vaughan's poem 'The Water-fall'[26] exhibits a still greater fascination with the natural world in its own right.[27] (No doubt Vaughan knew the numerous waterfalls of his own Welsh neighbourhood.) The poem, in due course, allegorises the waterfall and puts it to the use first of theology and then of spiritual discourse; but Vaughan begins with a liquid, verbal celebration of the place itself that reproduces its pause and rush and pause:

> With what deep murmurs through time's silent stealth
> Doth thy transparent, cool and watery wealth
>   Here flowing fall,
>   And chide, and call,
> As if his liquid, loose retinue stayed
> Ling'ring, and were of this steep place afraid,
>   The common pass
>   Where, clear as glass,
>   All must descend
>   Not to an end:
> But quickened by this deep and rocky grave,
> Rise to a longer course more bright and brave. (lines 1–12)

Vaughan continues (and shows his learning) by appealing to the principle of evaporation, in which the water, having reached the sea, will eventually return to the mountain top there to resume its descent. This is an affirmation of the hope of resurrection and, as such, a fairly predictable bit of theologising:

> What sublime truths, and wholesome themes,
> Lodge in thy mystical, deep streams! (lines 27–8)

At this point, the poem threatens to become banal and prosaic, but Vaughan turns it toward the inner life. It is not merely an intellectual knowledge he is longing for, but an interior, experiential, life-giving one. This knowledge is

> Such as dull man can never find
> Unless that Spirit lead his mind,
> Which first upon thy [the water's] face did move,
> And hatched all with his quickening love. (lines 29–32)

This new life, Vaughan hails as his true goal, one that eventually makes the merely this-worldly brook of little importance:

> O my invisible estate,
> My glorious liberty, still late!
> Thou art the channel my soul seeks,
> Not this with cataracts and creeks. (lines 37–40)

Elsewhere, we may find Vaughan more satisfied with visible, tangible nature. His poem ' "And do they so?" '[28] begins by citing Romans 8:19: 'For the earnest expectation of the creature waiteth for the manifestation of the sons of God.'[29] The poet then continues:

> And do they so? have they a sense
>   Of ought but influence?
> Can they their heads lift, and expect,
>   And groan too? why the elect
> Can do no more: my volumes said
>   They were all dull, and dead,
> They judged them senseless, and their state

Wholly inanimate.
Go, go; seal up thy looks,
    And burn thy books. (lines 1–10)

Later poets, too, are often unwilling to let the this-worldly, natural expression of the Spirit's life-giving grace disappear or be entirely subsumed within the other-worldly. Christopher Smart, with the Psalms as his model and David as his mouth-piece, celebrates the natural order as itself a prime manifestation of God's creative love:

He [David] sung of God – the mighty source
Of all things – the stupendous force
    On which all strength depends;
From whose right arm, beneath whose eyes,
All period, pow'r, and enterprise
    Commences, reigns, and ends.
        . . .
Glorious the sun in mid career;
Glorious th'assembled fires appear;
    Glorious the comet's train:
Glorious the trumpet and alarm;
Glorious th'almighty stretched-out arm;
    Glorious th'enraptured main.
                    ('A Song to David', stanzas 18, 84)[30]

At moments, Smart draws still nearer to non-human nature, almost dissolving the barrier of consciousness, as when he joins in his cat's feat of praising God by the mere action of being a cat:

For I will consider my Cat Jeoffrey.
For he is the servant of the Living God, duly and daily
    serving him.
For at the First glance of the glory of God in the East he
    worships in his way.
For is this done by wreathing his body seven times round
    with elegant quickness . . .[31]

The Romantics took the natural order with great seriousness as one of the points in human experience where we are open to the Holy. At times, they could write of it as if the moment of access were quite uncomplicated, as in the well-known sonnet of Wordsworth:

> It is a beauteous evening, calm and free,
> The holy time is quiet as a Nun
> Breathless with adoration; the broad sun
> Is sinking down in its tranquillity;
> The gentleness of heaven broods o'er the Sea:
> Listen! the mighty Being is awake,
> And doth with his eternal motion make
> A sound like thunder – everlastingly.
> Dear Child! dear Girl! that walkest with me here,
> If thou appear untouched by solemn thought,
> Thy nature is not therefore less divine:
> Thou liest in Abraham's bosom all the year;
> And worship'st at the Temple's inner shrine,
> God being with thee when we know it not.[32]

The 'mighty Being' with its thunder may easily be read first as the ocean, and Wordsworth makes no sharp distinction between the experience of ocean and the experience of God. Nor does he even require that the experience be conscious in order to have an effect on the human participant.

In Coleridge's *The Rime of the Ancient Mariner*, the encounter with God in nature is indeed conscious, but not, it would seem, voluntary. The sin of killing the albatross meets with its atonement only when the sailor, after long suffering and the death of all his comrades, receives the gift of recognising the beauty of the sea snakes:

> Beyond the shadow of the ship,
> I watched the water-snakes:
> They moved in tracks of shining white,
> And when they reared, the elfish light
> Fell off in hoary flakes.

> Within the shadow of the ship
> I watched their rich attire:
> Blue, glossy green, and velvet black,
> They coiled and swam; and every track
> Was a flash of golden fire. (Part IV)[33]

Yet these seem very like creatures from which he had earlier recoiled:

> The very deep did rot: O Christ!
> That ever this should be!
> Yea, slimy things did crawl with legs
> Upon the slimy sea.
>
> About, about, in reel and rout
> The death-fires danced at night;
> The water, like a witch's oils,
> Burnt green, and blue and white. (Part II)[34]

The difference seems to be less in the creatures themselves than in the mariner's sudden ability to see 'through' them to their God-given beauty:

> O happy living things! no tongue
> Their beauty might declare:
> A spring of love gushed from my heart,
> And I blessed them unaware:
> Sure my kind saint took pity on me,
> And I blessed them unaware.
>
> The self-same moment I could pray;
> And from my neck so free
> The Albatross fell off, and sank
> Like lead into the sea. (end of Part IV)[35]

Not only is the order of creation an expression of God's enduring grace, it actually fulfils a role in salvation, in the turning of the soul toward liberating intimacy with God.

The transparency of nature to God, at least as a possibility if not a predictable occurrence, became something of an article of faith in the English-speaking world after Wordsworth and Coleridge. Christina Rossetti, as a rather exacting Anglo-Catholic (and perhaps partly in reaction to the sensuousness of the pre-Raphaelites), is more wary. Yet she, too, could write of such an experience:

> A host of things I take on trust: I take
>> The nightingales on trust, for few and far
>> Between those actual summer moments are
> When I have heard what melody they make.
> So chanced it once at Como on the Lake:
>> But all things, then, waxed musical; each star
>> Sang on its course, each breeze sang on its car,
> All harmonies sang to senses wide awake.
> All things in tune, myself not out of tune,
>> Those nightingales were nightingales indeed:
>> Yet truly an owl had satisfied my need,
> And wrought a rapture underneath that moon,
>> Or simple sparrow chirping from a reed;
> For June that night glowed like a doubled June.[36]

For twentieth-century poets, the appeal to nature is perhaps less unambiguous. We feel compelled to acknowledge that nature may be violent and indifferent toward us – and that we have repaid the favour. Thus, Judith Wright's 'Cyclone and Aftermath'[37] begins with a powerful verbal image of the storm-winds' destructive passage through the trees:

> Hooded shadows out of a universe of weeping
> crouch on the gale through the rack of trees; repetitive
> of disaster, procession of fugitives. (lines 1–3)

The poem goes on to speak of the storm's danger to mariners, of the wreckage and decay it leaves behind it, and concludes by acknowledging the indifference of nature, creator of both serenity and distress – yet with the uneasy awareness that there is still more for us to plumb:

But look for her, too, when evening darkens and wind
    drops.
The shattered flowers melt into industrious earth;
the heron watches the pool, the high clouds stand
arena for the light's farewell. She is that figure
drawing the twilight's hood about her:
that wise woman from the land past joy or grief.

(lines 33–8)

Ultimately, nature is like every other point of access to God –
unpredictable. If its imagery is to serve the needs of spiritual
discourse, this, too, must be made clear. In R. S. Thomas's
'Suddenly',[38] the unexpected, unpredictable moment of intelligi-
bility affects not only the voice of nature, but that of all human
activity as well:

Suddenly after long silence
he has become voluble. (lines 1–2)

The address flows through water, leaves, rocks, weather, and
also human genes and skills. When all is said and done,
humanity is itself a part of nature. The result is a new Pentecost
of speech and understanding with

. . . weeds, stones, instruments,
the machine itself, all
speaking to me in the vernacular
of the purposes of One who is. (lines 22–5)

Of course, the implication of the creeds is that there can be no
sharp line between humanity and the rest of creation, but this
is a difficult point for us to accept. We always want to think of
ourselves as over against the rest of creation – a claim that
perhaps owes more to traditions of philosophy and theology
than to the Bible. Perhaps we have been most ready to see
humanity as continuous with nature in *childhood*, which forms
a minor but persistent theme in the poetic tradition.

Herbert could write that 'childhood is health'. But he was
writing specifically about the newly baptised infant:

> Oh let me still
> Write thee great God, and me a child . . .[39]

It was Vaughan, I believe, who first took the child per se as a kind of model of spiritual clarity and openness:

> Happy those early days! when I
> Shined in my Angel-infancy.
> Before I understood this place
> Appointed for my second race,
> Or taught my soul to fancy aught
> But a white, celestial thought . . .
>
> ('The Retreat', lines 1–6)[40]

Or, again:

> I cannot reach it; and my striving eye
> Dazzles at it, as at eternity.
>   Were now that chronicle alive,
> Those white designs which children drive,
> And the thoughts of each harmless hour,
> With the content too in my power,
> Quickly would I make my path even,
> And by mere playing go to Heaven.
>
> ('Childhood', lines 1–8)[41]

Thomas Traherne came to view the natural order as an intrinsic aspect of grace, both accessible to the human being and transparent to God – but with a transparency he had found available particularly in childhood:

> All appeared new, and strange at first, inexpressibly rare and delightful and beautiful. I was a little stranger, which at my entrance into the world was saluted and surrounded with innumerable joys. My knowledge was Divine . . . I saw all in the peace of Eden; Heaven and Earth did sing my Creator's praises, and could not make more melody to Adam, than to me. All Time was Eternity, and a perpetual Sabbath.
>   The corn was orient and immortal wheat, which never

should be reaped, nor was ever sown ... The dust and
stones of the street were as precious as gold ... The green
trees when I saw them first through one of the gates trans-
ported and ravished me.

These passages come from the prose meditations of Traherne's
Centuries, which also include a poem incorporating comparable
reflections. It concludes:

> Those thoughts His goodness long before
> Prepared as precious and celestial store:
> > With curious art in me inlaid,
> That childhood might itself alone be said
> > My tutor, Teacher, Guide to be,
> Instructed then even by the Deity.[42]

This view of the accessibility of God to human childhood
reappears in the works of William Wordsworth.[43] Like the
earlier authors, he saw childhood as the moment at which we
are closest and most open to the divine:

> Our birth is but a sleep and a forgetting:
> The Soul that rises with us, our life's Star,
> > Hath had elsewhere its setting,
> > And cometh from afar:
> > Not in entire forgetfulness,
> > And not in utter nakedness,
> But trailing clouds of glory do we come
> > From God, who is our home:
> Heaven lies about us in our infancy![44]

This interest in childhood, of course, is not merely abstract.
Vaughan and Traherne were seeking a kind of moral return
to childhood simplicity and delight. Wordsworth, perhaps less
optimistic in that regard, at least finds that the adult can retain
some blessing from an earlier, childhood nearness to the Holy
and gives thanks for:

> ... those first affections,
> Those shadowy recollections,

Which, be they what they may,
Are yet the fountain light of all our day,
Are yet a master light of all our seeing;
    Uphold us, cherish, and have power to make
Our noisy years seem moments in the being
Of the eternal Silence; truths that wake,
        To perish never;

. . .

    Hence in a season of calm weather
        Though inland far we be,
Our souls have sight of that immortal sea
        Which brought us hither,
    Can in a moment travel thither,
And see the Children sport upon the shore,
And hear the mighty waters rolling evermore.[45]

The poetic tradition is by no means unanimous in this high appraisal of childhood. Many of the poets are relatively indifferent to the subject, and, at the other extreme, John Betjeman's 'Original Sin on the Sussex Coast' makes a point of saying that children are as awful as other human beings. Judith Wright is particularly interesting in this regard. On the one hand, she shows a high regard for Thomas Traherne, not specifically for his treatment of childhood, but for his 'clear rejoicing'. It is a delight that, she believes, her own generation cannot comprehend.[46] At the same time, Wright sees children as becoming fully human through experience. According to 'Child with a Dead Animal', only the experience of loss prepares one for a fully human encounter with the Holy – and so for the Christian mysteries as well. The child's tears become its baptism:

They sign you Man, whose very flesh is made
of light's encounter with its answering shade.
    Take then this bread, this wine; be part of all.

                                        (lines 13–15)[47]

The materials of the poetic tradition we are examining are drawn from a variety of sources. We have looked particularly, in this chapter, at the ways in which the poets drew on scripture, the life of the church (particularly in worship) and the worlds of nature and human childhood for the language and imagery they might use to represent something that is classically deemed to be beyond ready human expression. To note the nature of this metaphoric and linguistic stock in trade is important, since, as we have acknowledged above, the medium and the message are always intimately interconnected. The poetry does not promise, in fact, that the reader will encounter God in the same ways, the same places – that is, in the natural world or in the church. Quite the contrary, it reaffirms that the Holy will meet us when it chooses, not just when we choose. And when it does so, the moment of meeting may well be neither in the church nor in the mountain, but in the midst of life's dailiness. Still, the choice of language and of image suggests a certain quality to the meeting and finds it equally at home in two realms of human experience: that of the Christian tradition and that of the natural world. Or to put the matter in more theological terms, nature and grace are both implicated in the realm of spirituality.

3. PRESENCE AND ABSENCE

Whenever human beings try to speak of the actual subject matter of spirituality, we move paradoxically beyond the capacities of ordinary human language, even of poetry. To complicate matters, there is a further paradox involved in trying to elucidate a poetic, metaphorical mode of discourse in prose, as I am doing here. What we can hope to find beyond the metaphor of the poem itself is not a pure philosophical discourse that can lay claim to a clarity of language without remainder. Quite the contrary, what lies beyond metaphor is that which cannot finally be spoken at all. Just as in the matter of love, where no other discourse could be said to capture the emotions of love as well as poetry and yet even the poetry of love cannot be said to be definitive or fully adequate to its topic, in the matter of spirituality, too, poetry cannot be surpassed and yet still falls short of its goal. It works allusively and metaphorically. It works by indirection, pointing the reader toward some moment of recognition that relates the poetic construct to the reader's own experience and helps the two to interpret one another or perhaps even opens up new realms of encounter with the Holy.

The aim, then, of a prose treatment, like this one, is not to 'explain' the poetry it refers to or to reduce metaphor to an unambiguous one-for-one clarity, but, at most, to clarify some obscurities on the level of the metaphors themselves and to help the reader sight along the trajectories of meaning created in the poems. What the reader will see along those trajectories will depend on her or his own experience as well as on skill in reading or alertness in moving beyond the surface of the text. It is impossible to deal with spirituality or the literature of spirituality entirely in terms of the intellect, particularly if we define the intellect, as we moderns often do, as a kind of computer inside the head. Spirituality always involves (though it is not limited to) experiences at the very edges or borders of our human reach. This border may, of course, be found at the heart of our lives as well as at their limits. The metaphorical 'mountain-top' takes many forms. But without cultivating this experience in the sense of seeking to understand it from within, no one can usefully enter into the discussion of spirituality. To think about spirituality seriously means to risk embarking on a voyage of discovery – a voyage whose precise dangers and destination you cannot know in advance. On this voyage, one learns something of oneself as well as of the spirituality of others.

PRESENCE

Despite the apparent absurdity of trying to leap at once to the very heart of our subject, we can best catch the unity of Anglican spirituality by beginning exactly there, by first locating the keystone of this spirituality and then seeing how other aspects serve to bridge to it, holding it in place while being held in place by it. While there is no single definitive way to describe this keystone experience, it is at least appropriate to speak of it in terms of a dialectic of absence and presence, an experience of the Holy, of God, that is both available and unavailable, both known and unknown, both intimate and distant, withheld at times and given at times. The transition from absence to presence, which I shall refer to here as 'the discovery of grace,' is the key experience around which Anglican poetic spirituality shapes itself.

Perhaps the experience of *absence* is the more usual for humanity. It may overtake us anywhere, at any time, as an experience of meaninglessness and futility. It may afflict us even in the midst of religious practice or the spiritual quest. In George Herbert's poem 'The Collar',[1] the speaker finds that it is exactly the most 'godly' element of his life that has come to seem pointless and, as a result, exhorts himself to abandon faith for pleasure:

> . . . leave thy cold dispute
> Of what is fit, and not. Forsake thy cage,
>   Thy rope of sands,
> Which petty thoughts have made, and made to thee
>   Good cable, to enforce and draw,
>   And be thy law,
> While thou didst wink and wouldst not see.
>   Away; take heed:
>   I will abroad. (lines 19–28)

The experience of religion has become an experience of meaningless restraints – cages and 'petty thoughts'. There is no meaningful presence here to make the voyage worthwhile.

Who is responsible for the absence? God or the speaker? It is difficult to say. Has the absence of God rendered the experience of faith dry? Or has the speaker's meddlesome and controlling religiousness masked the presence of God? In either case, the resolution of the predicament, the conversion from absence to presence, is initiated by God, not by the poetic voice:

> But as I rav'd and grew more fierce and wild
>   At every word,
> Me thoughts I heard one calling, *Child*:
>   And I replied, *My Lord*. (lines 33–6)

The overheard voice addresses the speaker in terms of family relationship: 'Child'. It makes the speaker's earlier sense of religious life as arbitrary convention and petty thoughts evaporate as it reasserts the presence of the Holy and reinstitutes the intimate, personal connection that makes faith a blessing instead of a curse. The speaker, unexpectedly, replies not 'Father', but 'My Lord'. There is an echo of 'Doubting' Thomas's 'My Lord and my God' – the words in which Thomas acknowledged the reality of Jesus' resurrection in John 20:28. This choice of language may be read as conventional piety, thus, in a way, reinstituting the whole religious system that the speaker was rebelling against. But even if it does return to the existing language of piety, it does so with a difference – namely, the discovery of grace, the re-opening of presence, the retrieval of life-giving possibility in relationship with God.

In this interchange, the speaker has become able to recognise the presence of the Holy again, but only through God's initiative in addressing him with a term of personal endearment (albeit one that suggests incomplete maturity). As a result, 'Lord' now means something far more than simply a pious, humble acknowledgement of God's greater power. It accepts the divine address to the speaker and embraces it as the foundation of the speaker's true life. The speaker's consent is not a return to the old religious life of cages and petty thoughts, even if his religious practice may remain largely the same. Instead, it is a return to intimacy. God's creative and searching love, expressed in the address 'Child', makes it possible for the speaker to address God as 'My Lord' in quite a different sense.

The poem's moment of discovery includes both a reunion with one's long-lost family and the return to delight in a life which had come to seem merely drab and difficult. The discovery of grace here is not an alteration in the external circumstances of life, but a transformation of perspective, what the New Testament writers call *metanoia* (often translated 'repentance' or 'conversion'). In the moment of *metanoia*, everything changes. One discovers that neither God nor world nor self is quite what one had thought. The discovery of grace affects everything.

The transformation wrought by grace is not always dramatic and instantaneous. It may be gradual and barely noticed at the time. Herbert suggests, in his poem 'The Holy Communion',[2] that there is an operation of grace on the whole person that is as hidden as the digestion of the eucharistic bread. Though he follows Paul's hierarchical description of the human being as composed of body, soul and spirit, he asserts that, at the communion, God approaches us even on the physical level – not through 'rich furniture, or fine array' (though these will have been found in many churches):

> But by way of nourishment and strength
>> Thou creep'st into my breast;
>> Making thy way my rest
> And thy small quantities my length;
> Which spread their forces into every part,
>> Meeting sin's force and art. (lines 7–12)

The bread, in and of itself, however, cannot affect the inner person. God must unlock the inner chambers of the soul to gain access to us. The grace of the sacrament effects this:

> Only thy grace, which with these elements comes,
>> Knoweth the ready way,
>> And hath the privy key,
> Op'ning the soul's most subtle rooms. (lines 19–21)

In and of themselves, these lines might be read as doing little more than versifying a traditional doctrine of sacramental grace. But they are doing that and more; they are leading toward a personal transformation, a discovery of grace that changes the world. Speaking of grace as knowing 'the ready way', having 'the privy key,' opening the 'most subtle rooms' is to speak of grace as lover. Eventually, this proffer of love on God's part reaches our spirit and transforms us so that we become as eager for the shared communication of love as God is. We no longer hide in the inner chamber, but go to the door to await the love letters we have come to expect:

> While those to spirits refin'd, at door attend
>> Dispatches from their friend. (lines 23–4)

To be the 'friend' of God here signifies the highest mark of grace. It is the title enjoyed by Abraham.[3] Yet, the point is not that it confers distinction, but that it reorients us. We now come to focus our attention on the absent friend with a confidence that 'dispatches' are on their way.[4]

The sense of new or renewed presence does not arise only out of the context of a prior sense of absence. It can also emerge as a moment of joy elevated by grace into ecstasy, as in Herbert's

'Easter (2)', quoted above.[5] Here the joy of the religious celebration of Easter morning gradually gives way to a moment of transcendence, a moment of extraordinary intimacy with God in the resurrection itself. Easter may be one day in the year; yet it is now, in truth, the only day that exists. Easter is one with eternity. In celebrating the religious feast, the speaker of the poem is surprised by an experience of the actual life of the resurrection and discovers that it already exists as the living reality that unites God and humanity. However many calendar days we live through, we are already in the eternal life of the age to come.

Such a transcendence of normal human limitations, in which one becomes aware of oneself as immersed in God or in eternity, is an aspect of what is commonly called mysticism.[6] The discovery of grace in Herbert and other Anglican poets may indeed sometimes take this form. It is, for example, hinted at in Christina Rossetti's sonnet, quoted in the previous chapter, which concludes:

> June that night glowed like a doubled June.[7]

As in Herbert's poem, the poet utilises the absurd language of a reality that is more than real. It is one of the ways mystics have of pointing toward an experience that is, in the strict sense of the word, ineffable.

Another way of speaking about mystical experience is in the language of the erotic. This has a long history in Christianity, going back to ancient readings of the Song of Songs or Song of Solomon. Without knowing the Song of Songs fairly well (preferably in the Authorised or King James Version of the Bible), it is easy for the reader to miss the frequency of reference to it in the tradition of English lyric poetry. Almost any reference to, for example, warm breezes, perfumes, enclosed gardens, the voice of the turtle (i.e. turtledove), harts, or lilies was likely to evoke this biblical text for the reader of another era. Henry Vaughan makes use of such allusions in 'The Revival'[8] to produce a poem that might seem only mildly erotic without the connection to Song of Songs – but the seventeenth-century reader is unlikely to have missed them:

Unfold, unfold! take in his light,
Who makes thy cares more short than night.
The joys, which with his *Day-star* rise,
He deals to all, but drowsy eyes:
And what the men of this world miss,
Some *drops* and *dews* of future bliss.
   Hark! how his *winds* have changed their *note*,
And with warm *whispers* call thee out.
The *frosts* are past, the *storms* are gone:
And backward *life* at last comes on.
The lofty *groves* in express joys
Reply unto the *turtle's* voice,
And here in *dust* and *dirt*, O here
The *lilies* of his love appear!

This poem does not have to be read as referring to mystical experience, to be sure. Can any writing be irrefutably interpreted as referring to something that mystics themselves say cannot be told? But the exuberant eroticism of the last couplet strongly suggests it. The fact that Vaughan located the lilies so emphatically in the dust and dirt, images of human mortality and sin, suggests the astonishment of this particular discovery of grace and the way in which it seemed to unite opposites. Vaughan insisted on referring to himself in quite negative terms as a sinner, and he appears to have been in frequent depression if not outright despair. On his tombstone, he asked to have carved the words *Servus inutilis, peccator maximus hic iaceo. Gloria. Miserere*: 'Here I lie, a worthless servant, the greatest sinner. Glory. Have mercy.'[9] For the lilies of God's love to appear in dust and dirt is precisely for the impossible to appear in the poet's own life.

While we cannot read poems as autobiography in any simple way, Vaughan is conceivably constructing a poetic counterpart to his own ecstatically bewildering and disorienting experience. He makes use of the ancient tradition of taking the female voice of the Song of Songs as an allegory of the human soul, which would encourage a certain use of female imagery (as conceived, of course, by a seventeenth-century male!) in the poet's mystical eroticism. One might see this at work in shaping the receptive opening line: 'Unfold, Unfold! Take in his light.' A similar eroticism pervades other Vaughan poems, for example 'The Morning Watch',[10] of which Stevie Davies has written, 'I hope it is not irreverent to call the poem's energy orgasmic.'[11] Indeed, any lesser term would be inadequate. Here, the common notion of the female as closer to nature is also apparent:

> O joys! Infinite sweetness! with what flowers,
> And shoots of glory, my soul breaks and buds!
>> All the long hours
>> Of night, and rest
>> Through the still shrouds
>> Of sleep, and clouds,
> This dew fell on my breast;
>> O how it *bloods*,
> And *spirits* all my earth! hark! In what rings,
> And *hymning circulations* the quick world
>> Awakes, and sings . . . (lines 1–11)

Thomas Traherne could also speak of the discovery of God's presence in intensely erotic terms. His poem 'Love'[12] is the more astonishing in that it moves from biblical imagery, more conventionally acceptable in such poetry, to classical allusions of divine–human eros, both heterosexual and homosexual:

> . . . Why, all power
>> Is used here
> Joys down from Heaven on my head to shower,
> And Jove beyond the fiction doth appear
>> Once more in golden rain to come
>> To Danae's pleasing fruitful womb.
>
> His Ganymede! His life! His joy!
> Or He comes down to me, or takes me up
>> That I might be His boy,

And fill, and taste, and give, and drink the cup.
      But these (tho great) are all
        Too short and small,
Too weak and feeble pictures to express
The true mysterious depths of blessedness.
      I am His image, and His friend.
      His son, bride, glory, temple, end. (lines 25–40)

The profusion of biblical images in the last two lines – and the slowing down of the lines themselves – brings the erotic enthusiasm to rest in a more generalised, but hardly less intense intimacy.

Another venerable way of gesturing toward mystical transcendence is the metaphor of inebriation;[13] yet another is to contrast it absolutely with the ordinary. Judith Wright does both in 'Grace':

Living is dailiness, a simple bread
that's worth the eating. But I have known a wine,
a drunkenness that can't be spoken or sung
without betraying it. Far past Yours or Mine,
even past Ours, it has nothing at all to say;
it slants a sudden laser through common day.

It seems to have nothing to do with things at all,
requires another element or dimension.
Not contemplation brings it; it merely happens,
past expectation and beyond intention;
takes over the depth of flesh, the inward eye,
is there, then vanishes. Does not live or die,
because it occurs beyond the here and now,
positives, negatives, what we hope and are.
Not even being in love, or making love,
brings it. It plunges a sword from a dark star.

Maybe there was once a word for it. Call it grace.
I have seen it, once or twice, through a human face.[14]

As Wright emphasises here, following the traditions of apophatic spirituality, words cannot capture mystical experience and human behaviours cannot force it. The most one can do is borrow metaphors and fling them, mixed with denials, in the direction of the ineffable.

I do not mean to say that the discovery of grace always implies the kind of experience usually called 'mysticism'. Our poets do not, in fact, seem very interested in categorising the various forms in which we encounter God's presence. What concerns them is the experience itself, the moment of discovery, whatever forms it may take. In *In Memoriam*, Alfred Tennyson's sense of the absence of God – indeed, the collapse of all meaning – is linked to the death of his beloved friend, Arthur Henry Hallam. His grief is intense, and the return of a sense of presence is gradual and unpredictable. One key moment is a dream narrative in poem lxix, which begins, in the garbled way of dreams, with an image of eternal winter in a busy, sooty urban environment. The dreamer escapes to the woods and there makes himself a crown of thorns. But wearing it brings him public reproach; he is called 'fool' and 'child'. Then

> I found an angel of the night;
> The voice was low, the look was bright;
> He look'd upon my crown and smiled:
>
> He reach'd the glory of a hand,
> That seem'd to touch it into leaf:
> The voice was not the voice of grief,
> The words were hard to understand. (lines 13–20)[15]

The new sense of presence here is ambiguous: 'the words were hard to understand'. Yet it is strong enough to appear as touch – not the touch of God, but that of a creature, specifically a male creature of low voice and bright look, whose gesture in some way parallels the lost love of Hallam. While the angelic interlocutor does not explain anything to the dreamer, he does, through his touch, give some hope of new life out of suffering. The crown of thorns, a sharing in Jesus' death, now becomes also a promise of sharing in Jesus' resurrection.

For Tennyson, given his loss, it may well be that a sense of God's presence without an accompanying sense of Hallam's would not be sufficient answer to the absence that afflicted him. This would not be unusual. Christians have often imagined the resurrection in terms of a great family reunion. Tennyson is at length able to find the two presences combined in poem cxxvi of *In Memoriam*:

> Love is and was my Lord and King,
>   And in his presence I attend
>   To hear the tidings of my friend,
> Which every hour his couriers bring.
>
> Love is and was my King and Lord,
>   And will be, tho' as yet I keep
>   Within his court on earth, and sleep
> Encompass'd by his faithful guard,
>
> And hear at times a sentinel
>   Who moves about from place to place,
>   And whispers to the worlds of space,
> In the deep night, that all is well.[16]

This discovery of grace is also a return: Love *is* and *was* my Lord and King. The love that drew him onward in his relationship with Hallam proves still to be alive with new possibilities, quite without denying the importance of the past. God is experienced as the one who unites the different episodes of the speaker's personal history. Though not what would usually be called 'mystical', it is a powerful rediscovery of a presence thought irretrievably lost in Hallam's death.

The discovery of grace is not just about the unexpected appearance of the Holy. It is also about the difficulties the self creates in its journey toward meaning. In 'The Revival', quoted above, Vaughan treats the renewal of presence as an act of God, discovered and accepted as soon as manifested. But it is not always so. It may also be that the human being resists God's gracious presence, even after it has been offered. Herbert devotes the third of the poems entitled 'Love'[17] to this aspect of discovering grace. This is the poem that concludes the main portion of his poetic collection *The Temple*, balancing 'The Altar' that opens it. Since both imply eucharistic references, one might well see 'Love' as the fulfilment of the promise of 'The Altar'. Here, God is all presence, all invitation; but the soul is afraid and long refuses to make itself present to the relationship offered by God:

> Love bade me welcome: yet my soul drew back,
>   Guilty of dust and sin.
> But quick-ey'd Love, observing me grow slack
>   From my first entrance in,
> Drew nearer to me, sweetly questioning,
>   If I lack'd anything.
>
> A guest, I answer'd, worthy to be here:
>   Love said, You shall be he.
> I the unkind, ungrateful? Ah my dear,
>   I cannot look on thee.
> Love took my hand, and smiling did reply,
>   Who made the eyes but I?
>
> Truth Lord, but I have marr'd them: let my shame
>   Go where it doth deserve.
> And know you not, says Love, who bore the blame?
>   My dear, then I will serve.
> You must sit down, says Love, and taste my meat:
>   So I did sit and eat.

Even when God is fully available, the human being is quite capable of avoiding the opportunity created by that presence. Perhaps the most insidious excuse is precisely the one of unworthiness, because it is founded in fact and supported by the traditions of Christian piety. Only God's persistence in inviting and inviting and inviting at length overcomes the speaker's refusal. The consummation of the invitation is phrased as simply as possible: 'So I did sit and eat.' The speaker takes the place reserved for a treasured guest, sits in the presence of God, and is fed. Here, the discovery of grace is less, it seems, a matter of mystical transcendence than of a long-denied consent to being loved.

NOW AND IN THE AGE TO COME

The discovery of grace belongs to the here and now. But the ultimate consummation of love and presence may be seen as belonging to the life of the age to come. John Donne's sacred poetry tends to speak of it as something to be hoped for anxiously after death; here, there is no chance of resting in God's presence. Yet, it is difficult to think that Donne looked toward the age to come with no foretaste of consolation in God's presence. His preaching has too much life and conviction for that to be the case. As he says in 'Hymn to God my God, in my Sickness',[18]

> And as to other souls I preach'd thy word,
>   Be this my Text, my Sermon to mine own,
>   Therefore that he may raise the Lord throws down.
>
> (lines 28–30)

Christina Rossetti also focused on the age to come as the moment of presence. Yet, this does not exclude present experience. One sonnet speaks of the partial present reward that will become full for the faithful only in the age to come:

> Love loveth Thee, and wisdom loveth Thee:
>   The love that loveth Thee sits satisfied;
>   Wisdom that loveth Thee grows million-eyed,
> Learning what was, and is, and is to be.
> Wisdom and Love are glad of all they see;
>   Their heart is deep, their hope is not denied;
>   They rock at rest on time's unresting tide,
> And wait to rest thro' long eternity.
> Wisdom and love and rest, each holy soul
>   Hath these today while day is only night:
>   What shall souls have when morning brings to light
>   Love, wisdom, rest, God's treasure stored above?

Palm shall they have, and harp and aureole,
Wisdom, rest, love – and lo! the whole is love.[19]

The sense of future promise is strong in the poem. Yet, on closer inspection, it appears that the joys of the age to come are in fact identical to those of the present – with the exception of the palm, harp and aureole. Indeed, 'the whole is love'. One recalls Paul's claim (1 Corinthians 13) that, though faith and hope will vanish in the age to come, love continues as the greatest of God's gifts. And the love of God experienced now is also the heart of experiencing God's presence in the age to come.

This hope in the age to come is not a rejection of present life. It looks toward a consummation of all human experience in the divine presence, including both present sorrow and present joy. Rossetti's 'A Rose Plant in Jericho',[20] in its first two stanzas, speaks of a complex life of delight and pain offered to God, with real but limited reward:

At morn I plucked a rose and gave it Thee,
A rose of joy and happy love and peace,
A rose with scarce a thorn:
But in the chillness of a second morn
My rose bush drooped, and all its gay increase
Was but one thorn that wounded me.

I plucked the thorn and offered it to Thee;
And for my thorn Thou gavest love and peace,
Not joy this mortal morn:
If Thou hast given much treasure for a thorn,
Wilt Thou not give me for my rose increase
Of gladness, and all sweets to me?

The thorn here reminds the reader of 'the thorn in the flesh' from which Paul prayed to be delivered (2 Corinthians 12:7). Yet, even it, when offered to Christ, yields the return of love and peace, though not of joy.

For the gift of an entire life, the speaker of the poem expects still larger increase – Christ's own self. Is this only in the age to come? The poet calls it 'Paradise', but that does not settle the question, for Paul was caught up into Paradise (2 Corinthians 12:4) in this life:

> My thorny rose, my love and pain, to Thee
>   I offer; and I set my heart in peace,
>   And rest upon my thorn:
>   For verily I think tomorrow morn
>   Shall bring me Paradise, my gift's increase,
> Yea, give Thy very Self to me.

In another poem (actually a pair of sonnets), titled with a borrowed Psalm verse, ' "Heaviness may endure for a night, but Joy cometh in the morning" ',[21] Rossetti speaks more clearly of a moment of presence in this life. Like the sonnet about the June evening at Como, it is connected with the natural world. The first sonnet begins as a night-time reflection on the futility of human life, which is then interrupted, in its closing sestet, by dawn and its accompanying chorus:

> Thus I sat mourning like a mournful owl,
>   And like a doleful dragon made ado,
>   Companion of all monsters of the dark:
> When lo! the light cast off its nightly cowl,
>   And up to heaven flashed a carolling lark,
>   And all creation sang its hymn anew. (lines 9–14)

The phrasing of the line 'the light cast off its nightly cowl' reveals the speaker's discovery that light is the fundamental reality, which does no more than disguise itself momentarily in the night. Such a discovery can only give rise to participation in the universal praise, as the beginning of the second sonnet makes explicit:

> While all creation sang its hymn anew
>   What could I do but sing a stave in tune? (lines 15–16)

RELUCTANCE

It must be said, of course, that the idea of entertaining God's presence is not always appealing. There is a danger, in that presence, that we may find ourselves confronted with a self we do not want to deal with; there is a fear that we may be overwhelmed by a power that does not really mean our good; there is even a certain bloody-mindedness that does not want to be bothered. The uncertainty is captured in a poem by Stevie Smith, whose work often suggests that she was both drawn and repelled by the figure of Jesus and by the Christian religion. In 'Who is This Who Howls and Mutters?'[22] the poetic voice speaks of a dispute with her muse – a divine figure – whom she sends away. The speaker expects the muse to argue with her, but, instead, the muse simply leaves. The poet searches for the absent inspiration, but without success until, at last, she appeals in ambiguous terms to one addressed as 'Lord'. The appeal is successful; and yet the muse's renewed presence turns out to be even more problematic for the poet:

> . . . Forgive me, Lord, I cry
> Who only makest Muses howl and sigh
> Thou, Lord, repent and give her back to me
> Weeping uncomforted, Lord have pity.
>
> He did repent. I have her now again
> Howling much worse, and oh the door is open.

(lines 19–24)

The presence of God is not all sweetness and light. It makes demands. Even in Herbert's 'Love (III)', the soul is compelled to deal with the fact that it uses its humility as a barrier against God's kindness, is compelled to decide whether it will become complicit in its own joy or hold to its wretched sense of selfhood. But what is the alternative? To avoid the presence of God does not protect us from such decisions. It only deprives us of a resource and a hope. T. S. Eliot captures the dilemma in the fourth section of *Little Gidding*, where he asserts that there is no alternative to suffering and that it is, in some indefinable way, the work of love:

> The only hope, or else despair
>   Lies in the choice of pyre or pyre –
>   To be redeemed from fire by fire.

> Who then devised the torment? Love.
> Love is the unfamiliar Name
> Behind the hands that wove
> The intolerable shirt of flame
> Which human power cannot remove.
>   We only live, only suspire
>   Consumed by either fire or fire. (lines 5–14)[23]

ABSENCE

The presence of God, then, may not be easy to choose, but when chosen it turns out to be the only true source of life. In the very nature of human life, however, God's presence is recognised only in relation to God's absence. Even if the joy of presence supervenes on the delights of a religious feast, as in Herbert's 'Easter (II)', quoted above, it may leave the carefully gathered boughs and sweets seeming pale by comparison. And any intense experience of the absence of God leads to pain and woe. In 'The Pulley', Herbert describes God as endowing the human being, in creation, with all possible riches, with the single exception of rest. God then gives this explanation for withholding that one gift:

> . . . let him keep the rest,
> But keep them with repining restlessness:
> Let him be rich and weary, that at least,
> If goodness lead him not, yet weariness
>   May toss him to my breast. (lines 16–20)[24]

Here Herbert, to be sure, puts a good face on it – in a kind of commentary on Augustine of Hippo's famous line: 'You have made us for yourself and our heart is restless till it rests in you.'[25] But absence is known as a pain that can be relieved only by the restoration of presence. If we acknowledge a value in it, it is only because it is a real and inevitable aspect of human experience, not to be sidestepped or denied, and because it holds out some strange, improbable hope of its opposite. Because one feels God's absence, one continues to think, almost involuntarily, that presence must yet be possible.

There is no single way to describe this pain – nor any endeavour to classify its different species. It makes itself known to us by many means. One is the experience of grief and loss. This is the mainspring of the dialogue with God in *In Memoriam*; and Tennyson begins the cycle of poems by asserting it. He begins by saying that he once agreed with an earlier poet,[26] who claimed

> That men may rise on stepping-stones
> Of their dead selves to higher things. (i, lines 3–4)

But he surrenders this hope in the light of his loss of Hallam. He feels that the only thing worth doing is at least to continue mourning the loss, to hang onto the absence as witness that Hallam was once present:

> But who shall so forecast the years
>   And find in loss a gain to match?
>   Or reach a hand thro' time to catch
> The far-off interest of tears?
>
> Let Love clasp Grief lest both be drown'd
>   Let darkness keep her raven gloss:
>   Ah, sweeter to be drunk with loss,
> To dance with death, to beat the ground,
>
> Than that the victor Hours should scorn
>   The long result of love, and boast,
>   'Behold the man that loved and lost,
> But all he was is overworn.' (i, lines 5–16).[27]

Given the central importance of Hallam for Tennyson, the loss of his beloved friend meant a general obscuring of his life – a loss of faith and of God's presence as well. In the Prologue to the cycle, he asks forgiveness for his grief, but describes it, significantly, as both 'what seem'd my sin in me' and as 'what seem'd my worth' (ll. 33, 34). After all, if he has confessed to absence, it was in order to be truthful to the presence that illuminated his life experience.

Tennyson's frankness in this regard was not revolutionary. He is preceded by the seventeenth-century poets who are equally frank about their occasions of disbelief and treat them as necessary or, at any rate, inevitable episodes in the human dialogue with God. Herbert's 'Affliction (I)'[28] is full of autobiographical elements suggesting that the argument with God that it contains is deeply informed by the poet's own internal struggles with God and with his vocation as a clergyman. The love affair with God, he says, began well enough with a sense of excitement and delight:

> When first thou didst entice to thee my heart,
> I thought the service brave:
> So many joys I writ down for my part,
> Besides what I might have
> Out of my stock of natural delights,
> Augmented with thy gracious benefits. (lines 1–6)

But all this eventually changed:

> At first thou gav'st me milk and sweetnesses;
> I had my wish and way:
> My days were straw'd with flow'rs and happiness;
> There was no month but May.
> But with my years sorrow did twist and grow,
> And made a party unawares for woe. (lines 19–24)

There followed sickness, the death of friends, a reluctant process of giving up public life, on which his heart was set, for the ordained ministry:

> I took thy sweeten'd pill, till I came near;
> I could not go away, nor persevere. (lines 47–8)

When all is said and done, the speaker feels himself trapped in a situation little to his liking, but without hope of leaving it – and, finally, without the desire to, since he is still drawn by the same love that he is rejecting:

> Now I am here, what thou wilt do with me
>   None of my books will show:
> I read, and sigh, and wish I were a tree;
>   For sure then I should grow
> To fruit or shade: at least some bird would trust
> Her household to me, and I should be just.
>
> Yet, though thou troublest me, I must be meek;
>   In weakness must be stout.
> Well, I will change the service, and go seek
>   Some other master out.
> Ah my dear God! though I am clean forgot,
> Let me not love thee, if I love thee not. (lines 55–66)

Herbert, of course, was placing this poem in the context of other 'sacred poems and private ejaculations,' as *The Temple* was subtitled. It is not the final word of his relation with God. But he makes no effort to sweeten *this* pill; he tells the unvarnished truth about the experience of absence that is integral to the experience of presence.

Grief appears elsewhere, too, as the trigger for the sense of absence. Elizabeth Barrett Browning, in 'De Profundis',[29] sketches a mental progress out of grief more pious than that of Tennyson, but not altogether unrelated to it. The speaker focuses first on loss and the seemingly interminable days that must now be got through without the absent beloved:

> The face, which duly as the sun,
> Rose up for me with life begun,
> To mark all bright hours of the day
> With daily love, is dimmed away –
> And yet my days go on, go on.

The tongue which like a stream could run
Smooth music from the roughest stone,
And every morning with 'Good day'
Made each day good, is hushed away –
And yet my days go on, go on. (stanzas i–ii)

Unlike Tennyson, in *In Memoriam*, Barrett Browning's speaker does eventually heed the rebuke against excessive grief, and finds that the seemingly endless extent of her grief is opened up into the eternity of the life of God, who teaches her, in the crucifixion, to surrender her attachment to grief:

By anguish which made pale the sun,
I hear him charge his saints that none
Among the creatures anywhere
Blaspheme against him with despair,
However darkly days go on.

– Take from my head the thorn-wreath brown,
No mortal grief deserves that crown.
O supreme Love, chief misery,
The sharp regalia are for *Thee*
Whose days eternally go on! (stanzas xix–xx)

Finally, the speaker is able to surrender absence to presence:

And, having in thy life-depth thrown
Being and suffering (which are one),
As a child drops some pebble small
Down some deep well and hears it fall
Smiling – So I! THY DAYS GO ON! (stanza xxiv)

Such confidence is not always possible. In Christina Rossetti's 'Confluents',[30] the promise of presence remains a question at the end. If the speaker of the poem continues to open and surrender the self to God even in absence, it is just that it is the one thing that she can in fact do. In this, she compares herself to the natural world of rivers and flowers and morning mists, suggesting that this is part of a larger pattern of reality:

As rivers seek the sea,
    Much more deep than they,
So my soul seeks thee
    Far away:
As running rivers moan
On their course alone,
    So I moan
    Left alone.

As the delicate rose
    To the sun's sweet strength
Doth herself unclose,
    Breadth and length;
So spreads my heart to thee
Unveiled utterly,
    I to thee
    Utterly.

As morning dew exhales
    Sunwards pure and free,
So my spirit fails
    After thee:
As dew leaves not a trace
On the green earth's face;
    I, no trace
    On thy face.

Its goal the river knows,
    Dewdrop finds a way,
Sunlight cheers the rose
    In her day:
Shall I, lone sorrow past,
Find thee at the last?
    Sorrow past,
    Thee at last?

The reiterations at the end of each stanza increase the sense of engagement and urgency. The fact that the final reiteration remains a question reveals the speaker's depth of uncertainty.

Even if our poets see absence as pointing toward presence, they cannot deny the depth of its attending distress.

The depth of that distress comes through clearly in John Donne, who seems, at least in his poetry, much more familiar with God's absence than with God's presence. In part, he sees this as a reflection of his own sinfulness; and others of our poets would agree that sin is an element in the human sense of distance from God. But the sense of absence is far more than that. It has to do with our finitude as creatures and with the sovereignty of the Holy, which places God beyond our control. We can plead, but we cannot command. Only God's habit of graciousness gives us assurance or even awakens the will to turn back to God. Thus, the fourth of Donne's 'Holy Sonnets':

> Oh my black Soul! now thou art summoned
> By sickness, death's herald and champion;
> Thou art like a pilgrim, which abroad hath done
> Treason, and durst not turn to whence he is fled,
> Or like a thief, which till death's doom be read,
> Wisheth himself delivered from prison;
> But damn'd and hal'd to execution,
> Wisheth that still he might be imprisoned.
> Yet grace, if thou repent, thou canst not lack;
> But who shall give thee that grace to begin?
> Oh make thyself with holy mourning black,
> And red with blushing, as thou art with sin;
> Or wash thee in Christ's blood, which hath this might
> That being red, it dyes red souls to white.[31]

A similar despair inhabits the 'terrible sonnets' of Gerard Manley Hopkins, a Roman Catholic by choice but a poet deeply imbued with the Anglican tradition we are discussing. He is, in this respect, the truest successor of Donne (though Donne moved in the opposite direction, from the Roman Church to the Church of England). He, too, identifies his sin as an element in his sense of distance from God. Yet, it is more than that; it is, for him, an inscrutable decree of God, who 'lives away' and does not answer correspondence and so condemns the speaker to misery:

I wake and feel the fell of dark, not day.
What hours, O what black hoürs we have spent
This night! what sights you, heart, saw; ways you went!
And more must, in yet longer light's delay.

With witness I speak this. But where I say
Hours I mean years, mean life. And my lament
Is cries countless, cries like dead letters sent
To dearest him that lives alas! away.

I am gall, I am heartburn. God's most deep decree
Bitter would have me taste: my taste was me;
Bones built in me, flesh filled, blood brimmed the curse.

Selfyeast of spirit a dull dough sours. I see
The lost are like this, and their scourge to be
As I am mine, their sweating selves; but worse.[32]

Bleaker than anything from Donne, this sonnet of Hopkins offers only one, back-handed element of hope. If the lot of 'the lost' is like this 'but worse', that holds out the faint promise that the speaker of the poem is not yet among them.

The absence of God leads us to besiege God with prayer – not the polite prayer of the pious, but the kind of prayer that bangs at the gates and demands relief from God's seeming aloofness. In the absence of the beloved friend, life loses its focus and purpose. Herbert is quite frank about such experience in 'Denial':[33]

When my devotions could not pierce
    Thy silent ears;
Then was my heart broken, as was my verse:
    My breast was full of fears
        And disorder.

My bent thoughts, like a brittle bow,
    Did fly asunder:
Each took his way; some would to pleasures go,
    Some to the wars and thunder
        Of alarms.

As good go anywhere, they say,
    As to benumb
Both knees and heart in crying night and day,
    Come, come, my God, Oh come,
        But no hearing. (lines 1–15)

The speaker of the poem reproaches God for creating humanity only to withdraw from us:

Oh that thou shouldst give dust a tongue
    To cry to thee,
And then not hear it crying! all day long
    My heart was in my knee,
        But no hearing.

Therefore my soul lay out of sight,
    Untun'd, unstrung:
My feeble spirit, unable to look right,
    Like a nipt blossom, hung
        Discontented. (lines 16–25)

After all this, the speaker is still left without answer, the final stanza of the poem being still a prayer for grace, not a celebration of its reception. The one sign of hope is the fact that, in this stanza for the first time in the whole poem, the last line rhymes with others instead of being left hanging and, as it were, out of tune:

Oh cheer and tune my heartless breast,
    Defer no time;
That so thy favours granting my request,
    They and my mind may chime,
        And mend my rhyme. (lines 26–30)

The absence of God turns out to be an absence also from our true self, which is brought into internal harmony only when it is also in life-giving relationship with its creator. Henry Vaughan, in 'The Pilgrimage',[34] describes the experience of absence in terms of the pilgrim who can see the desired, far-off goal, but is still far from reaching it. The poem begins with a description of a group of travellers making a night's stopover, their conversation focused only on where they have been and what they have seen there. The speaker of the poem, however, is eager for the morning and the chance to travel on. Unexpectedly, he begins to describe himself as a bird taken from its native ecosystem, never to be truly at home with its captors:

> I long, and groan, and grieve for thee,
> For thee my words, my tears do gush,
> *O that I were but where I see!*
> Is all the note within my bush.
>
> As birds robbed of their native wood,
> Although their diet may be fine,
> Yet neither sing, nor like their food,
> But with the thought of home do pine;
>
> So do I mourn, and hang my head,
> And though thou dost me fullness give,
> Yet look I for far better bread
> Because by this man cannot live. (lines 13–24)

We are not yet at home, as long as we live in the absence. We are not yet our true selves while our communion with God is thus compromised. To be aware of God's absence is to long for God's presence -- and not only God's presence, but the presence of our true life in our true world.

Christina Rossetti, in 'De Profundis',[35] suggests that, in the absence of the longed-for presence, one can sometimes do no more than reach for hope:

> Oh why is heaven built so far,
>   Oh why is earth set so remote?
> I cannot reach the nearest star
>   That hangs afloat.
>
> I would not care to reach the moon,
>   One round monotonous of change;
> Yet even she repeats her tune
>   Beyond my range.

> I never watch the scattered fire
>> Of stars, or sun's far-trailing train,
>
> But all my heart is one desire,
>> And all in vain:
>
> For I am bound with fleshly bands,
>> Joy, beauty, lie beyond my scope;
>
> I strain my heart, I stretch my hands,
>> And catch at hope.

Perhaps the supreme witness of absence among our poets is R. S. Thomas. The theme crops up again and again in his poetry. In 'In Church',[36] the absence seems unyielding, but the speaker of the poem has to attack it anyway. Like Thomas himself, the speaker appears to be a priest, lingering in the sacred space after the worshippers have departed. He describes the empty church as silent and lifeless. And in this apparently lifeless emptiness,

> ... There is no other sound
> In the darkness but the sound of a man
> Breathing, testing his faith
> On emptiness, nailing his questions
> One by one to an untenanted cross. (lines 16–20)

The speaker seems to expect no reply. The cross is empty. At best, this means that Jesus is risen. At worst, it means that he is gone entirely. Yet, he has questions that must be asked, that will not *not* be asked. If God chooses to remain silent in response, that will not keep the speaker from posing them.

Thomas can write of this absence as a kind of force in its own right, one that compels attention; indeed, the absence implies a presence of vital importance to him, however elusive it always seems to be. Absence is 'like a presence'. It is a place

> from which someone has just
> gone, the vestibule for the arrival
> of one who has not yet come.

> ('Absence', lines 5–7)[37]

Our inability to command a response remains, but also remains the evidence that a response is thinkable. More than thinkable – necessary, even; for the speaker of the poem finds he is unable to make sense of himself without it. Still, there is no assurance.

One might suspect that one's very sense of need is creating a false hope. Is the notion that someone is there to reply perhaps a fantasy? One must allow that possibility; yet, it does not remove the fascination or the expectation. In Thomas's 'Folk Tale',[38] alluding to stories like that of Rapunzel, the speaker admits that he is open to the charge that he has fantasised a presence in the tower; but he is still watching and waiting. Prayers, he says, are

> . . . like gravel
> > Flung at the sky's
> window . . . (lines 1–3)

The speaker would long ago have given up; but once he thought he saw

> the movement of a curtain. (line 16)

Sometimes in human experience the hope of presence is little more than this sense that the absence cannot be all, cannot be the whole story.

The alternation, then, of absence and presence, however unpredictable and seemingly arbitrary, has about it an inevitability. Like the alternation of day and night, of sleep and waking, of life and death and new life, the pain of absence and the joy of presence are related intimately to one another. Yet somehow, according to the poetic tradition, presence is still the goal; the presence of the lover, the beloved, is the ultimate word. Absence is actually ritualised in the church calendar, along with the corresponding promise of future presence. But that does not settle anything, as W. H. Auden reminds us:

> Will as we may to believe
> That parting should be
> And that a promise

Of future joy can be kept,
Absence remains
The factual loss it is . . .

('Ascension Day, 1964', lines 34–9)[39]

The promise does not keep the absence from being real. And
there is something in each of us that prefers it that way, that
cannot imagine any life-giving relationship with the Holy. While
absence and presence both have their power, however, the ultimate power belongs to presence, which threatens to overtake us
whether or not we believe 'that a promise/Of future joy can be
kept'.

In this alternation of absence and presence, the Anglican
poetic tradition identifies the central rhythm of Anglican spirituality. Absence may arise from a variety of causes – human
loss and grief, our own sin and weakness, the apparent refusal
of God to become available to us. And we may expect it to be
excruciatingly painful at times. To ignore it is a fool's solution.
The life-giving response is to look through it for the hope of
reunion:

Yet look I for far better bread
Because by this man cannot live.

(Vaughan, 'The Pilgrimage')

Suddenly after long silence
he has become voluble.

(Thomas, 'Suddenly')

The lofty *groves* in express joys
Reply unto the *turtle's* voice,
And here in *dust* and *dirt*, O here
The *lilies* of his love appear!

(Vaughan, 'The Revival')

While all creation sang its hymn anew
    What could I do but sing a stave in tune?

(Rossetti, 'Heaviness may endure . . .')

But I have known a wine,
a drunkenness that can't be spoken or sung
without betraying it. Far past Yours or Mine,
even past Ours, it has nothing at all to say;
it slants a sudden laser through common day.

(Wright, 'Grace')

Can there be any day but this,
Though many suns to shine endeavour?
We count three hundred, but we miss:
There is but one, and that one ever.

(Herbert, 'Easter (II)')

I am His image, and His friend.
   His son, bride, glory, temple, end.

(Traherne, 'Love')

4. LIVING BY GRACE

The dialectic of absence and presence lies at the heart of the poetic tradition in Anglican spirituality. But it is not the whole story. We might think of it as the 'soul' of this spirituality, the life-force that gives energy and movement to the rest. For the most part, however, the poets do not suggest that spirituality is merely to linger in the moment of presence. We participate in it fully; it gives us a new sense of connection with God and of being centred and oriented in our lives. But the enjoyment of presence is not the constant state of humanity here and now. It comes upon us, it does its work, we return to some less exalted state or even to the experience of absence. But we are transformed.

This is not to say that presence is limited to specially holy moments. As George Herbert urges, it can take up into itself the most everyday of tasks:

> A servant with this clause
> Makes drudgery divine:
> Who sweeps a room, as for thy laws,
> Makes that and th'action fine.

('The Elixir', lines 17–20)[1]

But we cannot make the enjoyment or even the pursuit of presence the entire definition of our lives, for it is not within our power to command grace even by our most dedicated seeking. As Judith Wright observes in a poem quoted in the preceding chapter:

> Not contemplation brings it; it merely happens,
> past expectation and beyond intention . . .
>
> ('Grace', lines 9–10)[2]

The dynamic created by the alternation of absence and presence is simply a defining fact of human existence. And the moments of presence are a glimpse or foretaste of fulfilment that reshapes our understanding of ourselves and our lives and gives direction to the living of those lives in their day-to-day orbits. The discovery of grace gives rise to a life lived by grace, and the poetic tradition has a good deal to say about the configuration of that life and about its inevitable limits.

SIN AND DEATH

Human life is not all sweetness and light. The discovery of grace does not alter this, but it makes possible a kind of searching and determined gaze that refuses to ignore or be deflected from examining the limitations of human life. Since life is made enormously rich by the experience of presence, there is no reason to pretend that everything is always fine in other respects. Human beings have limitations, both moral and practical, that prevent our building a perfect world for ourselves. Only our relationship with the Holy makes it possible to think in terms of a true richness of life and to begin the journey toward it – to start living by and from and for grace. Hence, there is no need to avoid the unpleasant topic of our weaknesses. Indeed, acknowledgement of them is a step toward genuine life.

One of the first things a modern reader of the Anglican poetic tradition is likely to notice is the attention it gives to these limitations, specifically in the forms of sin and death. Like all characteristics of the tradition, this one is not evenly distributed across the poetic landscape. It is particularly pronounced in the poets of the early and middle seventeenth century and again in some Victorian and modern writers. But its place in the tradition is perhaps magnified for the modern reader by the fact that we live in an era when it has long been unfashionable to talk about human sin or human limitations. This state of affairs, especially with regard to sin, is no doubt partly the fault of the churches, which have long trivialised the notion of sin by confining it almost entirely to the bedroom. It is also a product of modern progressivist notions that portray human life as moving rapidly and steadily onward and upward to greater and greater strength and wisdom. But it is also a massive act of denial on the part of our whole culture in a century characterised beyond all others by our massive destruction of one another and of the world in which we live. If we reject the words 'sin' and 'death' as encapsulating these realities of our experience, we shall have to find some others equally compelling. So far, they have not volunteered themselves.

The English Reformation's focus on sin and death probably owed much to medieval piety. One thinks, for example, of the importance of these themes to Julian of Norwich in her *Showings*. But it was also an expression of the Reformers' rediscovery of the centrality of grace. The Church of England was reluctant to write this discovery of grace into its formularies in the pervasive way that Lutheranism found in its 'grace alone' and 'faith alone', or the Reformed tradition in its doctrine of Double Predestination. Arguably, this was a good decision. It is not certain that clear definitions always help human beings discover grace at work in their lives. Indeed, Christians have been known to substitute allegiance to a definition for the grace to which it was supposed to point. Luther's doctrine of justification by grace alone through faith alone has not freed his successors from reconceiving faith itself as a form of works righteousness. And the Reformed tradition has turned out to be the fountainhead of most modern Christian fundamentalism with its attendant legalism.

Anglicanism made a modest salute to the doctrine of grace alone in its Thirty-Nine Articles.[3] It devoted its real energy to keeping sin and death in the public mind through writing them into the services of the church. Sin and death are not, to be sure, the point of the good news of grace; their importance is rather to reinforce our consciousness that the experience of God's presence depends on gift – which is to say on grace. Life and hope subsist in a generous relationship between God and the human being, not as the prize of purposive activity on our part. In other words, an awareness of sin and death is the best safeguard against the delusions of works righteousness, the fantasy that we are fully in charge of our own well-being.[4]

The confession of sin and prayer for mercy form as integral an aspect of the Anglican poetic tradition as of the services in the Book of Common Prayer. Robert Herrick's 'Prayer for Absolution'[5] applies the genre to his own poetry:

> For those my unbaptised rhymes,
> Writ in my wild, unhallowed times;
> For every sentence, clause and word
> That's not inlaid with thee, my Lord,
> Forgive me, God, and blot each line
> Out of my book that is not thine.
> But if, 'mongst all, thou findest here one
> Worthy thy benediction,
> That one of all the rest shall be
> The glory of my work and thee.

At first reading, the poem, coming near the beginning of his 'Noble Numbers', appears to be a kind of recantation for such 'unhallowed' (and more familiar) poems as 'Delight in Disorder' or 'To the Virgins, to Make Much of Time'. Yet Herrick actually published the 'Noble Numbers' as *part* of his *Hesperides*, the same collection that contained the more secular poems, and even dated them a year before the others. And the more 'secular' 'Hesperides' proper includes a number of religious lyrics.[6] Read in the light of that observation, 'His Prayer for Absolution' seems less a derogation of the non-religious works than an invitation to God to judge what is good and bad and a willingness to abide by the divine judgement.

This does not mean that Herrick's expression of repentance is insincere. There lies behind it a general acknowledgement of human sinfulness, including that of the author. But confession is never its own end. In the liturgy, confession of sin is always followed by the proclamation of absolution. Repentance looks to God's forgiving grace,[7] which actually makes room in it for a certain playfulness, such as we find in John Donne's 'A Hymn to God the Father'.[8] The speaker of the poem sounds a bit like Abram, bargaining with God over the fate of Sodom (Genesis 19:23–33). In the first two stanzas, every line or two raises the prospect of yet another kind of sin to be forgiven:

> Wilt thou forgive that sin where I begun,
>   Which is my sin, though it were done before?
> Wilt thou forgive those sins, through which I run,
>   And do run still: though still I do deplore?
>   When thou hast done, thou hast not done,
>   For I have more.
>
> Wilt thou forgive that sin by which I have won
>   Others to sin? and made my sin their door?
> Wilt thou forgive that sin which I did shun
>   A year, or two: but wallowed in a score?
>   When thou hast done, thou hast not done,
>   For I have more.

The whole third stanza, however, is devoted to a single sin, the sin of fear, which is, after all, one that cannot be dealt with effectively by forgiveness alone. God must do more – must alleviate it by the grace of God's presence.

> I have a sin of fear, that when I have spun
>   My last thread, I shall perish on the shore;
> Swear by thyself, that at my death thy son
>   Shall shine as he shines now, and heretofore;
>   And, having done that, Thou hast done,
>   I fear no more.

The poem constantly reiterates the same pun that links the verb form 'done' to the poet's name. God will 'have done' and 'have Donne' only when he opens Donne's heart to the assurance of divine grace (which itself makes an opportunity to pun on 'son' and 'sun'). The whimsy of such a prayer of repentance is not unserious. It takes sins quite seriously – above all the sins of doubt and fear and lethargy, the sins by which the speaker seems particularly separated from God's grace.

Henry Vaughan, as mentioned above, insisted that he be described on his tomb, in the churchyard at Llansantfraed, as *peccator maximus*, the greatest of sinners. His executors were apparently embarrassed by the request and prefixed the words: *Quod in sepulchrum voluit*, 'What he wanted on his tomb', making it clear to the passer-by that it represented Vaughan's own choice of words. But it is an apt representation of the way he saw himself – not as someone beyond hope, but as someone for whom hope was entirely dependent on grace. In 'Repentance',[9] what the speaker most repents is a tendency to despair of God's goodness. He admits that he has even turned God's grace into an imposition. He confesses that he routinely misapprehends God's goodness:

> My forward flesh creeped on, and subtly stole
> Both growth, and power; checking the health
> And heat of thine: that little gate
> And narrow way, by which to thee
> The passage is, he termed a grate
> And entrance to captivity;
> Thy laws but nets, where some small birds
> (And those but seldom too) were caught,
> Thy promises but empty words
> Which none but children heard, or taught.
> This I believed: and though a friend
> Came oft from far, and whispered, *No*;
> Yet that not sorting to my end
> I wholly listened to my foe.
> Wherefore, pierced through with grief, my sad
> Seduced soul sighs up to thee . . . (lines 5–20)

The misapprehension that makes of a 'gate' a 'grate' is enough to break off our communion with the Holy and make of life a desert.

The language the speaker uses here to characterise his folly may seem extravagant to the modern ear:

I am the gourd of sin, and sorrow
Growing o'er night, and gone to morrow,
In all this *round* of life and death
Nothing's more vile than is my breath,
Profaneness on my tongue doth rest,
Defects, and darkness in my breast,
Pollutions all my body wed,
And even my soul to thee is dead . . . (lines 71–8)[10]

The language is extreme – but precisely to identify the serious-ness of sin's consequences. Sin threatens to cut the speaker off from relationship with God and therefore from hope. The confession of this sin actually brings with it the hope of return through God's generous sharing of Godself through Christ:

Only in him, on whom I feast,
Both soul, and body are well dressed,
    His pure perfection quits all score,
    And fills the boxes of his poor;
He is the centre of long life, and light,
I am but finite, He is infinite.
O let thy *justice* then in him confine,
And through his merits, make thy mercy mine!

(lines 79–86)

Our own era does not want individuals to be weighed down by a sense of inadequacy or imperfection, something we are apt to call 'low self-esteem'. For that matter, great spiritual guides have long held that obsession with one's sinfulness is a spiritual disease, in its own right, reflecting a failure to trust God's saving generosity. In their different ways, both Donne and Vaughan seem to be making precisely this point. Their desire is to sur-render their inadequacies to God. They do not treat sin as the ultimate reality for human beings, but rather grace.

Sin remains powerful and, even if it is an unpopular category, it does not go away in later eras. What changes is not the reality of human wrongdoing, but our sense of where and how it is principally manifest. Given the new focus on nature in the poetry of William Wordsworth and Samuel Taylor Coleridge, the generalised sense of sin or the stress on doubt of a Donne or Vaughan was no longer specific enough. The destructive potential in humanity must be shown in relation to the larger world. The old sailor's painful history in Coleridge's 'The Rime of the Ancient Mariner'[11] is set in motion when he did the 'hellish thing' (line 91) of slaughtering, wilfully and without cause, the albatross that had become the gracious attendant of the ship. This was an act of spiritual refusal, rejecting the proffered opportunity to remain in communion with grace, manifested in this case by the bird's gift of companionship, at first hailed by the crew 'as if it had been a Christian soul' (l. 65). This is rejection of grace, the same sin of which Vaughan wrote, here manifested in Romantic terms by the killing of a free creature of the natural world.

In the twentieth century, W. H. Auden has been particularly insistent on sin as the human propensity to destroy both ourselves and others. In 'The Love Feast',[12] he borrows the image of the ancient Christian sacred meal of the same name to suggest that human sexuality has the possibility to connect us with grace or to refuse grace, that it can function as spirituality or as a parody of spirituality:

> In an upper room at midnight
> See us gathered on behalf
> Of love according to the gospel
> Of the radio-phonograph. (lines 1–4)

The speaker of the poem includes himself in the group. It is a statement about our shared humanity, not a declaration of moral superiority. The round of pursuit, rejection, betrayal, fear leads nowhere, but is difficult to escape. The speaker tries to leave, but sees the attractive 'Miss Number in the corner' and ends the poem with

> I am sorry I'm not sorry . . .
> Make me chaste, Lord, but not yet. (lines 27–8)

The poem finds its conclusion in the words of the young Augustine of Hippo,[13] who longed for the freedom and simplicity of chastity, but could not yet bring himself truly to choose it. Sin actually functions as a restriction on our freedom, frustrating our most deeply held desires.

The great sins of the twentieth century, however, have not been those of individuals, however destructive we may contrive to be by ourselves, but rather those of communities, fed by our capacity for mass self-delusion. The vast reach of that sin Auden pinpointed in 1937 in 'Danse Macabre',[14] in which a speaker who may be Death (or any of the strident, murderous ideologies of the mid-century) proclaims itself, in jangly lines, as the heir to humanity:

> It's farewell to the drawing-room's mannerly cry,
> The professor's logical whereto and why,
> The frock-coated diplomat's polished aplomb,
> Now matters are settled with gas and with bomb.
>
> (lines 1–4)

The Devil, the speaker plausibly argues, has been let loose on the world and his evil can only be stopped by the destruction of humanity – a consummation the speaker will shortly bring about:

> For it's order and trumpet and anger and drum
> And power and glory command you to come;
> The graves will fly open to let you all in,
> And the earth be emptied of mortal sin.
>
> The fishes are silent deep in the sea,
> The skies are lit up like a Christmas tree,
> The star in the West shoots its warning cry:
> 'Mankind is alive, but Mankind must die.'
>
> So good-bye to the house with its wallpaper red,
> Good-bye to the sheets on the warm double bed,
> Good-bye to the beautiful birds on the wall,
> It's good-bye, dear heart, good-bye to you all. (lines 49–60)

Here genocide, the greatest twentieth-century sin, paradoxically uses the more mundane human evils as a plausible excuse for itself.

There is no refuge from the mass evils of the twentieth century in a privileged realm of privacy. Our joint evil threatens our joint destruction, imaged in the stripped, totalitarian world Auden sketched in 'The Shield of Achilles':[15]

> A plain without a feature, bare and brown,
>   No blade of grass, no sign of neighborhood,
> Nothing to eat and nowhere to sit down,
>   Yet, congregated on its blankness, stood
>   An unintelligible multitude,
> A million eyes, a million boots in line,
> Without expression, waiting for a sign. (lines (9–15)

A sense of sin and the need for penitence are not irrelevant to our world, above all as regards our willingness to slaughter one another in the name of various pieties of religion, ethnicity and political ideology.

During World War I, Wilfred Owen produced a vivid image of the modern nation state living off the blood of its young while remaining conveniently unaware of what it has demanded of them. The poem is ironically entitled 'The Kind Ghosts',[16] but it appears that an earlier draft may have been called 'Britannia',[17] which identifies the female figure with whom the poem begins:

> She sleeps on soft, last breaths; but no ghost looms
> Out of the stillness of her palace wall,
> Her wall of boys on boys and dooms on dooms. (lines 1–3)

The comfortable oblivion of the state is its own ultimate sin, founded as it is on the massive destruction of the young, who turn out to be of no more consequence to the state than the decoration of its palaces.

The concern for such corporate sin was not new in the twentieth century but deeply rooted in the tradition. While earlier poems may be concerned more with the hidden sins of the individual soul and spirit, the denunciation of those who destroy

the commonweal for their own good goes back to Henry Vaughan
– and to one of his most famous poems, 'The World (I)':[18]

> I saw Eternity the other night
> Like a great *Ring* of pure and endless light,
>   All calm, as it was bright,
> And round beneath it, Time in hours, days, years
>   Driven by the spheres
> Like a vast shadow moved, in which the world
> And all her train were hurled . . . (lines 1–7)

The luminous image of the great ring of light, embodied perfectly in the sweep of the poem's opening rhythms, serves as
counterpoint to the shadow world of time and the self-absorbed
humans who are 'hurled' along in its train: the obsessed lover,
the 'darksome statesman', 'the fearful miser'. All these exclude
themselves from the bright ring by their self-obsession:

> Yet some, who all this while did weep and sing,
> And sing, and weep, soared up into the *Ring*,
>   But most would use no wing. (lines 46–8)

The singing and weeping go together, since the recognition of
one's failures, expressed in tears of repentance, goes hand in
hand with a willingness to rely on and rejoice in grace.

The attention paid to death in the poetic tradition is like that
paid to sin. It acknowledges human limitations and our con-
comitant need to seek – or, better, to wait on – the presence of
God and the grace that reorients us to our true life. Death is a
significant topic of meditation in the earlier poets, perhaps most
famously in John Donne's *Devotions upon Emergent Occasions*,
a series of meditations, expostulations, and prayers in highly
poetic prose, in which Donne reflects on death in the context of
his own near-fatal illness. The familiar seventeenth meditation[19] begins with the sick man hearing a passing bell tolled
at the parish church, announcing the departure of a parishioner,
and wondering about the identity of the dying person:

> Perchance he for whom this Bell tolls, may be so ill, as that

he knows not it tolls for him; and perchance I may think myself so much better than I am, as that they who are about me, and see my state, may have caused it to toll for me, and I know not that.

In due course, this brings the meditator to acknowledge our shared humanity in the face of death:

The Bell doth toll for him that thinks it doth; and though it intermit again, yet from that minute that that occasion wrought upon him, he is united to God. . . . No man is an island, entire of itself; every man is a piece of the Continent, a part of the main. If a clod be washed away by the sea, Europe is the less, as well as if a promontory were, as well as if a manor of thy friend's or of thine own were. Any man's death diminishes me, because I am involved in mankind. And therefore never send to know for whom the bell tolls; it tolls for thee.

What we often fail to notice in the passage is that this affirmation of human unity does not arise simply from our shared fate. It is grounded in the preceding appeal to grace, to the way in which God's goodness makes good our finitude:

The Church is Catholic, universal, and so are all her actions. All that she does belongs to all. When she baptizes a child, that action concerns me; for that child is thereby connected to that Head which is my Head, too, and engrafted into that body, whereof I am a member. And when she buries a man, that action concerns me. All mankind is of one Author and is one volume; when one man dies, one chapter is not torn out of the book, but translated into a better language; and every chapter must be so translated.

The acknowledgement of death is not simply a matter of stressing human weakness, but serves to redirect our attention toward the generosity of God which co-operates with us in the creation of a life that both accepts our limitations and transcends them. The earlier poets make this point explicitly, as in Robert Herrick's 'His Meditation upon Death':[20]

> Be those few hours, which I have yet to spend,
> Blest with the meditation of my end:
> Though they be few in number, I'm content;
> If otherwise, I stand indifferent:
>
>   . . .
>
> A multitude of days still heaped on,
> Seldom brings order, but confusion.
> Might I make choice, long life sho'd be withstood;
> Nor wo'd I care how short it were, if good:
> Which to effect, let ev'ry passing Bell
> Possess my thoughts, next comes my dolefull knell.
>
> (lines 1–4, 7–12)

There follows a meditation in which the bed and bed-clothes are likened to the grave and awakening to the resurrection, which in turn leads to judgement. This in turn prompts the desire for a life resistant to sin:

> Such let my life assure me, when my breath
> Goes thieving from me, I am safe in death;
> Which is the height of comfort, when I fall,
> I rise triumphant in my funeral. (lines 33–6)

In the later poets, one sometimes encounters a more brutally direct approach to the topic of death, perhaps in counterpoint to an increasing tendency in Victorian and modern times to pretend that it is not something we really have to deal with. The denial of death gets short shrift from Christina Rossetti in ' "Summer Is Ended" ':[21]

> To think that this meaningless thing was ever a rose,
>   Scentless, colourless, *this*!
>   Will it ever be thus (who knows?)
>   Thus with our bliss,
>   If we wait till the close?

> Tho' we care not to wait for the end, there comes the end
> > Sooner, later, at last,
> > Which nothing can mar, nothing mend:
> > > An end locked fast,
> > Bent we cannot re-bend.

Or, again, in a satirical poem without title:

> A handy Mole who plied no shovel
> To excavate his vaulted hovel,
> While hard at work met in mid-furrow
> An Earthworm boring out his burrow.
> Our Mole had dined and must grow thinner
> Before he gulped a second dinner,
> And on no other terms cared he
> To meet a worm of low degree.
> The Mole turned on his blindest eye
> Passing the base mechanic by;
> The Worm entrenched in actual blindness
> Ignored or kindness or unkindness;
> Each wrought his own exclusive tunnel
> To reach his own exclusive funnel.
>
> A plough its flawless track pursuing
> Involved them in one common ruin.
> Where now the mine and countermine,
> The dined-on and the one to dine?
> The impartial ploughshare of extinction
> Annulled them all without distinction.[22]

Here we have a sharp insistence on death as a fact that one cannot avoid and might better pay some attention to.

The twentieth-century world has evolved new skills and technologies for mass destruction that make death on a grand scale a more imminent threat, even while it remains an almost taboo topic. Judith Wright, in 'Request to a Year',[23] looks at this reality from a parental perspective, meditating on the kind of courage and acceptance necessary to send children out into the contemporary world. She relates a family story about her great-great-grandmother, 'legendary devotee of the arts', who found herself watching 'from a difficult distance' in the Alps a near fatal accident involving her son. Since she could nothing to help, she sketched the scene. The speaker of the poem concludes:

> Year, if you have no Mother's day present planned;
> reach back and bring me the firmness of her hand.

> (lines 21–2)

Wright describes her ancestor as having 'the artist's isolating eye' – not unrelated to the steady and determined gaze of a spirituality dependent on the discovery of grace. There is nothing that need be avoided or denied, since we already know that we are limited, in and of ourselves, and that our hope lies in our relatedness to God.

CREATIVE AND GRACEFUL LIVING

The life that is lived by grace is above all a life of creative response. The idea of living by rule is very common within Christianity, including Anglicanism. It may even be dominant. But it is not, as such, the life of grace. That is not to say that rules are useless, only that they are not supremely helpful. To live by grace is to have found grace at work in one's life and to respond by living that life actively with the power and direction that grace affords. Judith Wright embodies the energy of it in 'Prayer',[24] where she appeals for an old age that will not wane in creativity:

> And you, who speak in me when I speak well,
>   withdraw not your grace, leave me not dry and cold.
> I have praised you in the pain of love, I would praise you
>   still
> in the slowing of the blood, the time when I grow old.

> (lines 17–20)

Here the speaker of the poem appeals for a kind of personal intensity that is far from narcissistic. The poem affirms the reality of the world around her – a world that long preceded and will long follow the brief life of a single human being. Yet, the grace of the muse/God gives purpose and word that never cease to be worth our active engagement.

The life of grace is like the poetic experience of the muse – it flows from the divine communion of presence. Elizabeth Barrett Browning makes a similar comparison in 'A Musical Instrument',[25] which begins with the god Pan wrenching a reed from the waterside and transforming it with his knife into a flute. He is quite unaffected by the wreckage he leaves behind him:

> 'This is the way,' laughed the great god Pan,
>   (Laughed while he sate by the river!)
> 'The only way since gods began
> To make sweet music, they could succeed,'
> Then dropping his mouth to a hole in the reed,
>   He blew in power by the river.

The music the god makes, as it turns out, has the power to raise again what the god killed:

> Sweet, sweet, sweet, O Pan,
>   Piercing sweet by the river!
> Blinding sweet, O great god Pan!
> The sun on the hill forgot to die,
> And the lilies revived, and the dragon-fly
>   Came back to dream on the river.

But Pan cares nothing for the havoc he has caused. The difference in the God of grace, says Barrett Browning, lies not in causing less pain, but in grieving for it:

> Yet half a beast is the great god Pan
>   To laugh, as he sits by the river,
> Making a poet out of a man.
> The true gods sigh for the cost and the pain –
> For the reed that grows never more again
>   As a reed with the reeds of the river.

This is not to say that the life of grace is all extravert or productive in some obvious way. In fact, one effect of grace on us

is to make us stop and become more aware of the world in which
we live. R. S. Thomas contrasts that odd person who can stop
and contemplate with the busy crowd who avoid dealing with
reality by staying in constant motion:

> . . . There is always
> laughter out of the speeding
> vehicles for the man
> who is still, halfway though he be
> in a better direction.

> ('This One', lines 13–17)[26]

What the motorists cannot know is the life-giving quality of his
reflection, 'the green twig/with which he divines'.

The life of grace is not without pain, but it is a life marked by
new clarity and unexpected gifts. And the natural response to
these is praise – a life animated by praise and drawing its
strength from our moments of communion with the Holy. George
Herbert's 'The Elixir'[27] is a classic statement of it:

> Teach me, my God and King,
>   In all things thee to see,
> And what I do in anything,
>   To do it as for thee:
>
> Not rudely, as a beast,
>   To run into an action;
> But still to make thee prepossessed,
>   And give it his perfection.
>
> A man that looks on glass
>   On it may stay his eye;
> Or if it pleaseth, through it pass,
>   And then the heav'n espy.
>
> All may of thee partake:
>   Nothing can be so mean,
> Which with this tincture (for thy sake)
>   Will not grow bright and clean.

> A servant with this clause
> Makes drudgery divine:
> Who sweeps a room, as for thy laws,
> Makes that and th'action fine.
>
> This is the famous stone
> That turneth all to gold:
> For that which God doth touch and own
> Cannot for less be told.

The poet borrows the language of alchemy to say that the life of grace is the same life as any human being lives, yet transformed by the perspective in which it is seen. Life as gift of grace, as means of communion, is golden, whatever its specific content or status.

INCARNATION IN THE EVERYDAY

Anglicanism has been described as having a strong doctrinal focus on the Incarnation. Certainly, the poetic tradition in our spirituality takes a highly incarnational approach to human existence. God's presence is not something to be sought outside of ordinary human existence by means of heroic practices of prayer or asceticism or learning. It is something to be recognised under our very noses – the difference between looking at a piece of glass, in the poem of Herbert just quoted, or through it. When all is said and done, this is achieved in the context of quite ordinary existence or it is not really achieved at all. This means that the life of grace is supremely accessible, as near as one's own life or that of any neighbour.

Tennyson speaks of the Incarnation in precisely such terms. The message of grace Jesus brings is not unprecedented; it is deeply implicit in our creation. But it is given new currency for us:

> Tho' truths in manhood darkly join,
> Deep-seated in our mystic frame,

We yield all blessing to the name
Of Him that made them current coin;

For Wisdom dealt with mortal powers,
    Where truth in closest words shall fail
    When truth embodied in a tale
Shall enter in at lowly doors.

And so the Word had breath, and wrought
    With human hands the creed of creeds
    In loveliness of perfect deeds,
More strong than all poetic thought;

Which he may read that binds the sheaf,
    Or builds the house, or digs the grave,
    And those wild eyes that watch the wave
In roarings round the coral reef.[28]

What neither philosophy nor poetry can make accessible, a life can. If Tennyson writes here specifically of the life of Jesus, the same principle may be applied more broadly.

Matthew Arnold, in 'The Buried Life',[29] wrote of the way revelation can occur in the intimate relationship of lovers as well. The poem begins with the speaker complaining to the beloved of the shallowness of their interchange, which only masks deeper concerns:

Light flows our war of mocking words, and yet,
Behold, with tears mine eyes are wet!
I feel a nameless sadness o'er me roll. (lines 1–3)

The sadness, as the poem pursues it, turns out to be the basic human longing to know one's true life:

But often, in the world's most crowded streets,
But often, in the din of strife,
There rises an unspeakable desire
After the knowledge of our buried life;
A thirst to spend our fire and restless force
In tracking out our true, original course;

> A longing to inquire
> Into the mystery of this heart which beats
> So wild, so deep in us – to know
> Whence our lives come and where they go.
> And many a man in his own breast then delves,
> But deep enough, alas! none ever mines. (lines 45–56)

To reach something of one's own truth is not, finally, possible in isolated search. What it requires is the rare moment of communion when we find ourselves most truly incarnate in our own being because of another's loving touch:

> Only – but this is rare –
> When a belovéd hand is laid in ours,
> When, jaded with the rush and glare
> Of the interminable hours,
> Our eyes can in another's eyes read clear,
> When our world-deafen'd ear
> Is by the tones of a loved voice caress'd –
> A bolt is shot back somewhere in our breast,
> And a lost pulse of feeling stirs again.
> The eye sinks inward, and the heart lies plain,
> And what we mean, we say, and what we would, we know.
> A man becomes aware of his life's flow,
> And hears its winding murmur; and he sees
> The meadows where it glides, the sun, the breeze.
>   . . .
> And then he thinks he knows
> The hills where his life rose,
> And the sea where it goes. (lines 77–90, 96–8)

The essential point here is the emphasis on human communion. Arnold makes no reference to grace, to God, to revelation in a religious sense. The 'belovéd hand' one takes to be that of a human lover. Yet the result is a vision of self that is far from merely secular, a vision that sees the self in relation to its beginning and ending.

Love is the essence of human communion, whether with God

or with another human being, and our poetic tradition has constantly related the two to one another. One may distinguish sacred and profane loves,[30] but they can also intermingle and inform one another. Robert Herrick's 'To God'[31] is a kind of love-song:

> Come to me, God; but do not come
> To me, as to the gen'ral Doom,
> In power; or come Thou in that state,
> When Thou Thy laws didst promulgate,
> Whenas the Mountains quak'd for dread,
> And sullen clouds bound up his head.
> No, lay thy stately terrors by,
> To talk with me familiarly;
> For if thy thunderclaps I hear,
> I shall less swoon than die for fear.
> Speak thou of love and I'll reply
> By way of *Epithalamy,*
> Or sing of mercy, and I'll suit
> To it my Viol and my Lute:
> Thus let Thy lips but love distil,
> Then come, my God, and hap what will.

Some of Herrick's phrasing here may seem a trifle daring, but he was prepared to go further and relate the love of God to the love – even the sexual love – of human beings for one another.

Herrick's reference to 'epithalamy' or marriage ode evokes echoes of the Song of Songs. It also reprises a theme found elsewhere in his poetry, notably in 'Julia's *Churching, or Purification'*.[32] The overt subject of the poem is the rite of 'churching of women', by which a woman was restored to public life after her confinement in childbirth and gave thanks for her survival and that of the child. As Douglas Brooks-Davies has pointed out,[33] Herrick placed the poem in close proximity to poems concerned with Candlemas (February 2), which is the Feast of the Purification of the Virgin and of the Presentation of Jesus in the Temple. In this way, he links the contemporary experience of marriage and childbearing to the divine action of incarnation.

The poem, in fact, does this in a rather bawdy way, even though it begins with a sober and religious picture adorned with details drawn from the Old Testament rather than from seventeenth-century church life:

> Put on thy *Holy Fillitings,* and so
> To th'Temple with the sober *Midwife* go.
> Attended thus (in a most solemn wise)
> By those who serve the Child-bed mysteries,
> Burn first thine incense; next, whenas thou see'st
> The candid stole thrown o'er the *Pious Priest,*
> With reverend curtsies come, and to him bring
> Thy free (and not decurted) offering.
> All Rites well ended, with fair Auspice come
> (As to the breaking of a Bride-Cake) home:
> Where ceremonious *Hymen* shall for thee
> Provide a second *Epithalamy.*
> *She who keeps chastely to her husband's side*
> *Is not for one, but every night his Bride:*
> *And stealing still with love and fear to Bed,*
> *Brings him not one, but many a Maiden-head.*

The references to the bride's chastity suggest images of the marriage of God and God's people or of Christ and the individual soul, both common interpretations of Song of Songs; reference to her ongoing virginity connects her with Mary, whose feast has just been celebrated. Yet, the poem ends with an explicit celebration of married sexual love. Herrick was taking incarnation quite seriously.

John Donne also used the liberty granted by an incarnate spirituality to speak to God in a lover's terms. In the thirteenth of his 'Holy Sonnets', he describes the 'picture of Christ crucified':

> Tears in his eyes quench the amazing light,
> Blood fill his frowns, which from his pierc'd head fell.

He perceives this face as beautiful and goes on to ask himself:

And can that tongue adjudge thee unto hell,
Which pray'd forgiveness for his foes' fierce spite?
No, no; but as in my idolatry
I said to all my profane mistresses,
Beauty of pity, foulness only is
A sign of rigour: so I say to thee,
To wicked spirits are horrid shapes assign'd.
This beauteous form assures a piteous mind.[34]

The next sonnet in the sequence continues the sexual metaphor with a plea to God to claim the speaker of the poem as God's own. It even concludes with the disturbing metaphor of rape:

Take me to you, imprison me, for I
Except you'enthrall me, never shall be free,
Nor ever chaste, except you ravish me.[35]

The intensity of Donne's engagement with God has about it here an element of violence that is not common in the poetic tradition of Anglican spirituality. It does, however, seem integral to Donne's own spirituality, a tension of powerful oppositions and conflicting desires that finds itself particularly at home in such outrageous expression.

If sexual metaphor can be used to talk about the incarnate quality of spirituality, it is because the sexual is inherently related to the spiritual. Both concern themselves, at their best and healthiest, with communion. Every human communion involves the Holy in some way or other. W. H. Auden captures a moment of spiritual transparency that might have any of a variety of sources, observed in a New York cafe shortly after the end of World War II:

Having finished the Blue-plate Special
And reached the coffee stage,
Stirring her cup she sat,
A somewhat shapeless figure
Of indeterminate age
In an undistinguished hat.

When she lifted her eyes it was plain
That our globular furore,
Our international rout
Of sin and apparatus
And dying men galore,
Was not being bothered about.

Which of the seven heavens
Was responsible her smile
Wouldn't be sure but attested
That, whoever it was, a god
Worth kneeling-to for a while
Had tabernacled and rested.

('In Schrafft's')[36]

The anonymity of the woman's epiphany may be embarrassing to those who see Christianity primarily in terms of the boundaries of the church. But Auden was not the first to say that love as such is fundamental to the God-given, grace-filled experience of life.

Christina Rossetti, who was a rigorous Anglo-Catholic and exacting about matters of church rites, could write about the centrality of love in terms that have little religious specificity to them:[37]

If love is not worth loving, then life is not worth living,
    Nor aught is worth remembering but well forgot;
For store is not worth storing and gifts are not worth
        giving,
    If love is not;

And idly cold is death-cold, and life-heat idly hot,
And vain is any offering and vainer our receiving,
    And vanity of vanities is all our lot.

Better than life's heaving heart is death's heart
        unheaving,
    Better than the opening leaves are the leaves that rot,

For there is nothing left worth achieving or retrieving,
    If love is not.[38]

This is a negative statement, to be sure, simply asserting the fundamental necessity of love and not defining its forms. But Rossetti, for all her otherworldliness, was prepared to link the human and divine loves in significant ways. One example is the poem 'Doeth well . . . doeth better'.[39]

My love whose heart is tender said to me,
    'A moon lacks light except her sun befriend her.
Let us keep tryst in heaven, dear Friend,' said she,
    My love whose heart is tender.

From such a loftiness no words could bend her:
    Yet still she spoke of 'us' and spoke as 'we',
    Her hope substantial, while my hope grew slender.

Now keeps she tryst beyond earth's utmost sea,
    Wholly at rest, tho' storms should toss and rend her;
And still she keeps my heart and keeps its key,
    My love whose heart is tender.

Here the human love of two people for one another is also the power that sustains the weaker of the two, the one more given to despair, in the hope of presence.

No question but that this high valuation of human love is difficult for the tradition to sustain – even in the context of an Anglican ecclesiastical tradition that committed itself, at the Reformation, to a belief in the sacredness of marital sexuality. Wilfred Owen was perhaps responding to the continuing taboo against same-gender love in 'Maundy Thursday'.[40] He depicts the rite of veneration of the cross:

Between the brown hands of a server-lad
The silver cross was offered to be kissed. (lines 1–2)

The different members of the congregation greet the cross with varying understandings, but the poet chooses a different object of veneration:

(I kissed the warm live hand that held the thing.) (line 14)

The church, it seems, wants the ritual object preferred to the human hand. In reversing this valuation, the poet asserts the divine value incarnate in human flesh itself.

In 'Maundy Thursday', the poet seems prepared to abandon the divine love for the human. In other poems, he speaks in a less polarised way, acknowledging a certain interpenetration between the two, though he continues to express suspicion of the church – the 'disciples' and 'priests' and 'scribes' of the poem 'At a Calvary near the Ancre':

> One ever hangs where shelled roads part.
>   In this war He too lost a limb,
> But his disciples hide apart;
>   And now the Soldiers bear with Him.
>
> Near Golgotha strolls many a priest,
>   And in their faces there is pride
> That they were flesh-marked by the Beast
>   By whom the gentle Christ's denied.
>
> The scribes on all the people shove
>   And bawl allegiance to the state,
> But they who love the greater love
>   Lay down their life; they do not hate.[41]

In the desperate realities of the war, true access to the presence – and absence – of God belongs to those most deeply implicated, to the soldiers who incarnate the present human distress, not to the professional servants of religion.

COMMUNITY

Since living in grace means living incarnate in human flesh, it also inevitably means living in human community – with, we hope, a new and more generous awareness, commitment and purpose. There is no humanity without community: we are made human by it, we contribute to its character, we bring others into it. The meditation by John Donne quoted above is a favourite example of this theme in the poetic tradition, but it is far from isolated.

Henry Vaughan was supremely conscious of the power and necessity of human connectedness – the way in which others give us much of who we are. He expressed it most intensely in relation to those he had lost to death. In 'Joy of my life! while left me here',[42] he begins by lamenting a particular loss (either his wife or his twin brother) but then frames more widely both the debt and the hope that these human connections bestow:

> Stars are of mighty use: the night
>   Is dark, and long;
> The road foul, and where one goes right,
>   Six may go wrong.
>   One twinkling ray
>   Shot o'er some cloud,
>   May clear much way
>   And guide a crowd.
>
> God's saints are shining lights: who stays
>   Here long must pass
> O'er dark hills, swift streams, and steep ways
>   As smooth as glass;
>   But these all night
>   Like candles, shed
>   Their beams, and light
>   Us into bed.
>
> They are (indeed) our pillar-fires
>   Seen as we go,
> They are that City's shining spires
>   We travel to:
>   A swordlike gleam
>   Kept man for sin
>   First *out*; this beam
>   Will guide him *in*.

Our connection with Adam means that humanity has been

shut out of Eden. But the connection with our saints (and the individuality of the lament suggests that these are Vaughan's quite personal saints) restores us to paradise.

Vaughan was most aware of the importance of community when it was broken. But he also saw in it the arena for the restoration of our true humanity. In 'Faith',[43] he speaks of faith as a divine gift that creates a new and broader human family:

> Bright, and blest beam! whose strong projection
>   Equal to all,
> Reacheth as well things of dejection
>   As the high, and tall;
> How hath my God by raying thee
>   Enlarged his spouse,
> And of a private family
>   Made open house!
> All may be now co-heirs; no noise
>   Of *bond*, or *free*
> Can interdict us from those joys
> That wait on thee . . . (lines 1–12)

The poem refers to the enlargement of the household of Israel by inclusion of Gentiles in the church. The rejection of the distinction between bond and free is also rooted in the New Testament, where it plays a role in early baptismal teaching.[44] But the poem implies that these are living effects of faith, not merely historical facts.

The importance of the doctrine of the Incarnation for Anglicanism has been most apparent in precisely this tendency to emphasise the social aspect of human and spiritual experience. God becomes accessible in and through our shared humanity. Hence William Blake's perfectly orthodox location of 'The Divine Image' in humanity:

> To Mercy Pity Peace and Love
> All pray in their distress,
> And to these virtues of delight
> Return their thankfulness.

For Mercy Pity Peace and Love
Is God our father dear,
And Mercy Pity Peace and Love
Is Man his child and care.

For Mercy has a human heart,
Pity, a human face,
And Love, the human form divine,
And Peace, the human dress.

Then every man of every clime
That prays in his distress,
Prays to the human form divine,
Love Mercy Pity Peace.

And all must love the human form
In heathen, turk or jew.
Where Mercy Love & Pity dwell
There God is dwelling too.[45]

Blake certainly had doubts about the degree to which this hope was realised in humanity (and specifically in the church). He etched, but did not publish, its counterpart in *Songs of Experience*:

Cruelty has a human heart,
And Jealousy a Human Face . . .[46]

But this is simply to underline his own recognition, rooted in the biblical teaching about the image of God in humanity and in Jesus' teaching of love, that there is no authentic human spirituality that does not express itself in love of neighbour, in recognition of our common and divine humanity.[47]

The upheaval and distress of technological change, already begun in Blake's time and continuing throughout the nineteenth century, joined with democracy, nationalism, and other forces, practical and ideological, to create the turbulent era in which we still live. If the poets' awareness of the social world was serious, it could hardly ignore all this or avoid trying to discern its link to the spirit's conversation with God. Elizabeth

Barrett Browning was a particular exponent of this theme, perhaps most notably in her verse novel *Aurora Leigh*, the length of which places it outside the materials for this study. It is also the theme of the shorter, but interlinked, poems of 'Casa Guidi Windows'. Having written, with deep engagement, on contemporary political events in Florence (and in some respects found herself too optimistic in her evaluation of them), Barrett Browning turns, at the end, to a spiritual foundation for hope. She summons her two-year-old child to

> . . . be God's witness – that the elemental
>   New springs of life are gushing everywhere
> To cleanse the water courses, and prevent all
>   Concrete obstructions which infest the air!
> – That earth's alive, and gentle or ungentle
>   Motions within her, signify but growth;
> The ground swells greenest o'er the labouring moles.
>   Howe'er the uneasy world is vexed and wroth,
> Young children, lifted high on parent souls,
>   Look round them with a smile upon the mouth,
> And take for music every bell that tolls.
>   Who said we should be better if like these?
> And we sit murmuring for the future though
>   Posterity is smiling on our knees,
> Convicting us of folly? Let us go –
>   We will trust God. The blank interstices
> Men take for ruins, He will build into
>   With pillared marbles rare, or knit across
> With generous arches, till the fane's complete.
>   This world has no perdition, if some loss.
>   (Part 2, stanza xxv, lines 20–39)[48]

This is not easy optimism, but a hard-won hope, linked here to Jesus' teaching about becoming like children, but made the poet's own by the intense struggle of the earlier poems in the collection.

In the twentieth century, the hope may have become more

difficult, but it survives if only in the form of a prayer from the trenches, as in Wilfred Owen's 'Nocturne':[49]

> Ah! I should drowse away the night most peacefully
> But that there toil too many bodies unreposed
> Who fain would fall on lethargy. (lines 11–13)

This prayer for others' sleep recognises the human unity that Donne captured in saying that 'No man is an island'. But this unity also robs sleep of its promise, whether in the form of the poet's responsibility for the men under his command 'who fain would fall on lethargy' or simply because his awareness of the precariousness of all human life brings him back to his own sleep-robbing uncertainty.

Our true community, indeed, is broader than just the human one. William Wordsworth found a kind of moral imperative for humanity in the natural world. In 'Lines Written in Early Spring',[50] the fact that we are part of nature, part of a much larger reality, serves to condemn our treatment of one another:

> I heard a thousand blended notes,
> While in a grove I sate reclined,
> In that sweet mood when pleasant thoughts
> Bring sad thoughts to the mind.
>
> To her fair works did Nature link
> The human soul that through me ran;
> And much it grieved my heart to think
> What man has made of man. (lines 1–8)

Community with the universe makes demands on us.

It also gives gifts. Judith Wright has written, in 'Night Herons',[51] of the way in which a moment in the natural world can create human community:

> It was after a day's rain:
> the street facing the west
> was lit with growing yellow;
> the black road gleamed.

First one child looked and saw
and told another.
Face after face, the windows
flowered with eyes.

It was like a long fuse lighted,
the news travelling.
No one called out loudly;
everyone said 'Hush'.

The light deepened; the wet road
answered in daffodil colours,
and down its centre
walked the two tall herons.

Stranger than wild birds, even,
what happened on those faces:
suddenly believing in something,
they smiled and opened.

Children thought of fountains,
circuses, swans feeding;
women remember words
spoken when they were young.

Everyone said 'Hush';
no one spoke loudly;
but suddenly the herons
rose and were gone. The light faded.

In this most apocalyptic of centuries, the hope that human
community might actually be realised may itself take on apocalyptic tones – but in terms of the apocalyptic of fulfilment that
points to a hope beyond the apocalyptic of seemingly unending
tribulation. R. S. Thomas, in 'A Country',[52] has written of such a
vision or imagination, one that gives life meaning even as it
falls far short of attaining:

It is nowhere,
            and I am familiar

with it as one is
with a song.
>>I know its background,
>>>the terraces
of cloud that are the hanging gardens
>>>of the imagination.
No sun
>>rises there, so there is no sun
to set. It is the mind
suffuses it with a light
>>that is without
>>>shadows.
>>>>Invisible fountains
play, though their skirts
are of silk.
>>And who lives there,
you ask, who walks
its unmetalled highways?
>>It is a people
who pay their taxes
>>in poetry; who repair broken
names; who wear the past
as a button-hole at their children's
>>marriage with what is to be.

ACCEPTING SURPRISE

The poetic tradition we are tracing here is not uniform. I make
no assumption that, if we could put all our poets into one room
together, they would find themselves in prose agreement. What,
then, justifies calling this a tradition? To some extent, we might
say that it is simply the shared recognition of membership in a
particular historical community – one that has sought to 'pay
its taxes', to deliver up what is necessary for the life of the
whole. I have argued that the Anglican poetic tradition has a
language formed in worship and bespeaks both a spirituality
concerned with the inner life of the individual and a spiritu-

ality that begins and ends in the community. But the tradition is not defined in a simple way by any one of these things.

This spirituality does, however, have a centre to which all these elements relate. It is this centre that qualifies it to be thought of as a spiritual tradition and not just an assemblage of individual reflections. The centre is surprise. Our poets are interested in the ways that God surprises us, changes our minds, brings about conversion and change. They return again and again to the discovery and rediscovery of grace, the unpredictable, unfathomable and, indeed, humanly impossible moment of recognising and assenting to God's goodness. Sometimes this takes the form of a kind of mystical self-transcendence, but not always. Most of the time, it takes the simpler form of a somewhat embarrassed encounter with delight that casts all of life in a new light. Often it is not specifically religious at all, as in Judith Wright's lines quoted above:

> Stranger than wild birds, even,
> what happened on those faces:
> suddenly believing in something,
> they smiled and opened.

But whether the language is specifically religious or not, the point is the surprise itself, the unexpected encounter with grace. In 'Night Herons', the gift of presence disappears as suddenly and without warning as it came. It is always beyond human control. In R. S. Thomas's words:

> Suddenly after long silence
> he has become voluble.[53]

Neither the silence nor the unexpected communication can be managed or scheduled or even predicted. They always come by way of surprise.

Not only is the word from God a surprise. So is the rare moment when we find in ourselves the grace to acknowledge and accept. George Herbert's 'Love (III)', quoted in the previous chapter, creates an image of God's insistent return to the soul, appealing, inviting, welcoming, and of the soul's bewilderment at being brought to the table and its final, reluctant, half-doubting consent. This poem forms the conclusion and, arguably, the climax of *The Temple*. After it, come only the word 'FINIS' and the inscription: 'Glory be to God on high, and on earth peace, good will towards men', drawn from the canticle sung after receiving communion in the Book of Common Prayer as Herbert knew it.[54]

But the question is whether the speaker will in fact accept the proffered nourishment at all. Love is all assurance and kind solicitude, but the speaker is anxious and ashamed. The speaker, aware of God's loving approach, wants not to accept but to escape it, would hang onto the identity of unworthy outsider rather than become a welcome guest. However absurd this may seem, it is an entirely familiar human response to God's love. And it is only with great difficulty that God's loving tact at last breaks through the speaker's reserve. The surrender is conveyed in the most succinct, abashed manner: 'So I did sit and eat.' But, after all the resistance, those few words capture the liberating improbability of the moment, the astonishing surprise of the grace that allows us to accept grace. The deepest surprise is not only that one is welcomed, but that one becomes free to accept the welcome.

This surprise of grace lies at the heart of the Anglican poetic tradition. It lies there because of George Herbert more than anyone else, since it figures so prominently in his poems. His emphasis on surprise does not discount other aspects of life. He urges a responsible, moral life in *The Temple's* prefatory poem, 'The Church Porch', and he concludes *The Temple* by returning from the paradise of 'Love (III)' to the relatively mundane ecclesiastical concerns of 'The Church Militant'. But the surprise of grace is the heart of the whole collection, appearing over and over in a variety of ways. Herbert does not merely assert its importance. He models it again and again in the little world of the individual poem. He invites the reader to become one with the speaker of the poem, to hear the invitation, to resist, and, when all the resources of resistance are exhausted, to consent.

But that consent surprises us with the gift of full intimacy with God.

Alfred Tennyson recounts a comparable, but far slower progression toward the acceptance of grace in *In Memoriam*. It is a progression lost on most readers today, who know the work only through excerpts in anthologies. For the reader concerned with spirituality, this is an occasion of regret, for the work as a whole is stronger than any of its parts. It is possible for the more optimistic and hopeful poems in the cycle, when read in isolation, to seem shallow in a way that they do not in context, since they emerge out of the grief that gave them their original significance. Hallam's death shook Tennyson not only by the personal loss, but also because he found he had no very persuasive context of faith or knowledge in which to understand it. By attending carefully and honestly to the pain of his years of grief and to the ways his spirit dealt with it, he arrived at a point of acceptance that could transcend the grief without denying or abandoning it. Grace here is not the sudden shock of Herbert or Vaughan, but it is nonetheless a surprise, dawning more gradually in the soul and embraced only as the stronger storms of grief begin to subside.

The consent to grace, of course, is not inevitable. It is not common for the earlier poets to explore the implications of refusing rather than consenting. This becomes a task more for the twentieth century, bursting through, for example, in Wilfred Owen's 'The Parable of the Old Man and the Young'.[55] The title of the poem refers to Jesus' parables and therefore alerts the reader to see it as a story in which one will find (or perhaps lose) oneself, one's soul. The story itself is taken from Genesis 22, but it catches the reader with an unexpected twist:

> So Abram rose, and clave the wood, and went,
> And took the fire with him, and a knife.
> And as they sojourned both of them together,
> Isaac the first-born spake and said, My Father,
> Behold the preparations, fire and iron,
> But where the lamb, for this burnt-offering?

Then Abram bound the youth with belts and straps,
And builded parapets and trenches there,
And stretchèd forth the knife to slay his son.
When lo! an Angel called him out of heaven,
Saying, Lay not thy hand upon the lad,
Neither do anything to him, thy son.
Behold! Caught in a thicket by its horns,
A Ram. Offer the Ram of Pride instead.

But the old man would not so, but slew his son,
And half the seed of Europe, one by one.

By his choice of where to begin the story, Owen avoids ascribing
the original motivation of the sacrifice to God,[56] but the reader
will remember that part of it, since it is one of the great scandals
of scripture. Abram, then, is acting in the service of religion; but
this does not bring him any closer to grace. The abrupt transition makes the binding of Isaac virtually a response to the
child's temerity in questioning his father. We have a hint in
the 'belts and straps', the 'parapets and trenches' that Owen
has something in mind beyond a simple retelling of the story.
Yet, it is still a shock to discover in the final two lines that the
determination to do the act that one has duly and religiously
settled on has led not only Abram, but Western humanity generally, to reject the gracious voice from heaven and so to destroy
its own children. The refusal of grace is mortal – not only for the
refuser but for everyone in the refuser's power.

In the twentieth century, as belief has become both more
needful and less easy, at least for those attentive to the horrors
of our era, the surprise of grace is not easy to write about
persuasively. But it remains the mainspring of the Anglican
poetic tradition. The distance that resides inside us as well as
outside, making us reluctant to consent to grace even when it
is offered – this distance fuels the spiritual longing, and its
resolution is, of all the secrets of human inwardness, perhaps
the most difficult to convey. Above all, grace still comes as a
surprise, as in R. S. Thomas's 'Arrival':[57]

Not conscious
　　that you have been seeking
　　　　suddenly
　　you come upon it

the village in the Welsh hills
　　dust free
　　with no road out
but the one you came in by.

　　A bird chimes
from a green tree
the hour that is no hour
　　you know. The river dawdles
to hold a mirror for you
where you may see yourself
　　as you are, a traveller
　　　　with the moon's halo
　　above him, who has arrived
　　after long journeying where he
　　　　began, catching this
　　one truth by surprise
that there is everything to look forward to.

One inevitable characteristic of a spirituality of surprise is
that it cannot offer anyone much in the way of a concrete map
for reaching the goal. Anglican spirituality, taken in the larger
sense, has its map-makers: prose writers like Jeremy Taylor
and William Law. Herbert himself was willing to sketch a sort
of poetic instruction to the young ('Perirrhanterium', which
makes up most of 'The Church Porch', prefixed to *The Temple*)
in which he instructs them about the basic duties of life and
religion. Such works are full of good advice about responsible
behaviour and a proper religious valuing of human life. But
there is no pretence that they can somehow bring one to the
moment of surprise. Only God can do that. This is a spirituality,
then, of recognition, not of preparation. It does not give you a
map for getting there, only a set of images that may help you

interpret the place and experience when you do. T. S. Eliot's famous lines from *Little Gidding* are of use only to those who are already experiencing what he speaks of:

We shall not cease from exploration
And the end of all our exploring
Will be to arrive where we started
And know the place for the first time.

(V, lines 26–9)[58]

Perhaps the best the tradition can offer by way of a spiritual *paideia* is in fact the reading of poetry, which implies also the cultivation of an awareness that there is something beyond language, a something toward which the most powerful language, with all its resources of sound, rhythm and metaphor, only gestures. Such an awareness may make us a little quicker to sense the divine glance. Nothing can 'make' the surprise of grace happen. For that, we rely on the purposes of a God understood in Christian faith as Love. But the mode of attentiveness that poetry cultivates can perhaps make us more alert. In any case, the poets provide us with abundant companionship along the way.[59]

THE PERILS OF RELIGION

A spirituality of surprise cannot offer a 'how-to'. It must, in fact, be very modest about what it can offer. Spirituality does not confer ownership of the Holy. The most spiritually advanced of human beings remain profoundly ignorant of God. George Herbert's poems suggest a life in which one is surprised not once but repeatedly by God's graceful interventions. We never come to be in possession of the reality about God in a way that would insulate us from surprise, from the shock of the unexpected or the risk of conversion and change. The arrogance that too easily attaches to religion is sharply bracketed and relativised in the poetic tradition, knowing as it does how easily God can subvert our most strongly held preconceptions. The poetic tradition assumes a humility that can pay attention to actual experience and place it in conversation with the tradition rather than merely strait-jacketing it in doctrine.

George Herbert, for example, begins the main section of *The Temple* with the emblematic poem 'The Altar',[60] which suggests from the beginning that the exercise of religion and the spirituality of the heart are related, but not identical:

> A broken ALTAR, Lord, thy servant rears,
> Made of a heart, and cemented with tears:
>   Whose parts are as thy hand did frame;
>   No workman's tool hath touch'd the same.
>   A   HEART   alone
>   Is   such   a   stone,
>   As   nothing   but
>   Thy pow'r doth cut.
>   Wherefore each part
>   Of my hard heart
>   Meets in this frame,
>   To praise thy name.
>   That if I chance to hold my peace,
>   These stones to praise thee may not cease.
> Oh let thy blessed SACRIFICE be mine,
> And sanctify this ALTAR to be thine.

Whether we conceive of the altar so described as a literal object, created in accordance with the Torah's prohibition of hewn stones, or as an image of Herbert's poetical work here embodied in a book, the poem both parallels and contrasts it with the primary work of the heart, which is the truest possible site for the worship of God.[61]

This is not to suggest that the poetic tradition in Anglican spirituality is inevitably opposed to organised religion – only that it lives in an uneasy relationship with it, aware that religion is always in danger of the root sin of idolatry, of worshipping and offering for worship itself rather than the unknowable God who surprises us with grace. Surprise, after all, is not a convenient, long-term foundation for an institution. Only if

religion can contrive to remain transparent to grace, can it serve
the needs of spirituality well. And sometimes, for some people,
it does so. Thomas Traherne, for example, in 'Christmas-Day',
is able to make a quite direct connection between the church
bells and the heart's praise:

> At break of day, O how the bells did ring?
> > To Thee, my King,
> > The bells did ring;
> > To Thee the angels sing:
> Thy goodness did produce this other spring,
> For this it is they make the bells to ring:
> > The sounding bells do through the air
> > Proclaim Thy welcome far and near;
> > While I alone with Thee inherit
> > All these joys, beyond my merit.
> > > Who would not always sing
> > > To such a King? (lines 85–96)[62]

But the connection is seldom so direct and is sometimes
hard to make at all. Henry Vaughan wrote most of his poetry
during the Commonwealth, when the worship he had known
and been fed by was proscribed. In 'Religion',[63] he writes of the
Christian faith as something that is grace-filled in principle,
but hardly in the form in which he then encountered it. The
poem begins by evoking the image of a grove, whose leaves,
as gradually becomes apparent, are the pages and stories of
scripture:

> My God, when I walk in those groves,
> And leaves thy spirit doth still fan,
> I see in each shade that there grows
> An Angel talking with a man
>
> Under a *juniper*, some house,
> Or the cool *myrtle's* canopy,
> Others beneath an *oak's* green boughs,
> Or at some *fountain's* bubbling eye;

Here *Jacob* dreams, and wrestles; there
Elias by a raven is fed . . . (lines 1–10)

The poet then questions why there seems to be so little such intimacy with God in his own day and concludes that religion and its corruption are at fault:

. . . Religion is a spring
That from some secret, golden mine
Derives her birth, and thence doth bring
Cordials in every drop, and wine;

But in her long, and hidden course
Passing through the earth's dark veins,
Grows still from better unto worse,
And both her taste and colour stains,

Then drilling on, learns to increase
False *echoes*, and confusèd sounds,
And unawares doth often seize
On veins of *sulphur* under ground;

So poisoned, breaks forth in some clime,
And at first sight doth many please,
But drunk, is puddle, or mere slime
And 'stead of physic, a disease;

Just such a tainted sink we have . . . (lines 29–45)

Vaughan was writing about a fundamentally anti-Anglican religious establishment. But that is not to say that Anglicanism is free of the capacity to work comparable harm. William Blake wrote of the propensity of religion as such, especially the established religion of the Church of England, to place itself between the believer and grace. In fragments called 'The Everlasting Gospel', which he did not complete or publish, he used an astute reading of the gospels to attack the religion of his day, which he saw as being dedicated to enforcing morality and teaching the lower classes the duty of subservience. All this, he claims, is in sharp contrast to what Jesus did and taught:

If Moral Virtue was Christianity
Christ's Pretensions were all Vanity,
And Caiaphas & Pilate, Men
Praise Worthy . . .
The Moral Christian is the Cause
Of the Unbeliever & his Laws. (frag. 1, lines 1–4, 7–8)
. . .
Then Jesus rose & said to Me,
'Thy Sins are all forgiven thee.'
Loud Pilate Howl'd, loud Caiaphas yell'd
When they the Gospel Light beheld.
It was when Jesus said to Me
'Thy Sins are all forgiven thee.' (frag. 2, lines 17–22)
. . .
If he had been Antichrist, Creeping Jesus,
He'd have done any thing to please us:
Gone sneaking into Synagogues,
And not us'd the Elders & Priests like dogs,
But Humble as a Lamb or Ass
Obey'd himself to Caiaphas. (frag. 3, lines 55–60)[64]

The references here to synagogues, Caiaphas, Pilate, and so forth seem rather thinly veiled allusions to the church and government of Blake's own time.

For Blake, religion as he knew it seems to have been primarily a barrier to spiritual awareness, to a meeting with the Holy. What is worse, it was a barrier imposed deliberately by self-interested and prurient clerics:

I went to the Garden of Love,
And saw what I never had seen:
A Chapel was built in the midst,
Where I used to play on the green.

And the gates of this Chapel were shut,
And, 'Thou shalt not' writ over the door;
So I turn'd to the Garden of Love
That so many sweet flowers bore;

And I saw it was filled with graves,
And tomb-stones where flowers should be;
And Priests in black gowns were walking their rounds,
And binding with briars my joys & desires.

('The Garden of Love')[65]

Here, the locked chapel exists only to occupy and command the space that had formerly been open to a playful encounter with the natural world. This is no accident, as its clergy devote themselves to the further restriction of whatever might be left outside their control. The finality of their control is emphasised, in the closing couplet, by the sudden metrical change from three-beat to four-beat lines.

Blake's antagonism toward organised religion – including his use of the figure of Jesus as a foil to Christianity – has had its successors. Stevie Smith, whose poetry often struggles with and rejects traditional Christianity,[66] finds the figure of Jesus much more interesting, spiritually, and contrasts him with what religion subsequently makes of him. In 'The Airy Christ',[67] she describes Jesus as looking 'aloofly down', knowing that he is destined to suffering and defeat and that 'the words he sings' will be turned into rules – rules that tone-deaf people will pretend to hear as music. The speaker warns the reader against such folly:

Heed it not. Whatever foolish men may do the song is cried
For those who hear, and the sweet singer does not care
    that he was crucified.

For he does not wish that men should love him more than
    anything
Because he died; he only wishes they would hear him sing.
    (lines 15–18)

For Smith, it seems, the Christian religion makes 'working laws' out of Jesus' song and pretends to hear music it is deaf to. It would be difficult to argue that the charge is entirely untrue.

On the other hand, Christian religion may be helpful to the spiritual journey if it is understood principally not in terms of doctrinal hair-splitting or moral disapproval or the maintenance of a set of institutions, but as a community of those looking to be surprised by grace, listening for the music that is often drowned out by the noise of our daily preoccupations, and learning to live in the conviction that these things and not the 'working laws' are central. Hence, even though Blake and Smith may have separated themselves from the church, it does not follow that their poetry falls outside the tradition of Anglican spirituality. Quite the contrary, they represent a significant aspect of it always in danger of being lost – the conviction that the church, the religion, is not God.

The spiritual journey that takes one away from the more conventional pieties of the church, however, is not inherently safer than the one that stays within it. Tennyson recognises this in *In Memoriam*. On the one hand, he is prepared to insist on the value of doubt and continued enquiry. On the other, he recognises his sister's more conventional, less questioning faith as the equal of his own:

> O thou that after toil and storm
>   Mayst seem to have reach'd a purer air,
>   Whose faith has centre everywhere,
> Nor cares to fix itself to form,
>
> Leave thou thy sister when she prays,
>   Her early heaven, her happy views;
>   Nor thou with shadow'd hint confuse
> A life that leads melodious days.
>
> Her faith thro' form is pure as thine,
>   Her hands are quicker unto good:
>   Oh, sacred be the flesh and blood
> To which she links a truth divine!
>
> See thou, that countest reason ripe
>   In holding by the law within,
>   Thou fail not in a world of sin,
> And ev'n for want of such a type. (xxxiii)[68]

The fact that the speaker's sister 'leads melodious days' and that 'Her hands are quicker unto good' than his suggests to him that the religious differences between them are not the real issue. If traditional religion is not a guarantee of spiritual awareness, neither is the questioning of such religion. However much the poet has moved forward along the path that Hallam's death determined for him, he has no guarantee that this will automatically translate itself into a life lived by the grace he has been discovering.

The religion of the Church of England, then, has had an ongoing role to play in the generation of the poetic tradition in its spirituality; yet it cannot be said to 'own' the tradition or to confine it within its own boundaries. Indeed the tradition itself has had an effect in broadening Anglicanism's sense of itself. This may be partly because, after Donne and Herbert, almost all of the major voices in this tradition have been those of lay persons with no particular burden on them to maintain the official stance of their church. When Tennyson writes about the church of his day, it is in a tone of some dismissiveness. A friend and partisan of the theologian F. D. Maurice, he writes to him at a time when Maurice was suffering accusations of unorthodoxy and invites him to visit the Tennysons on the Isle of Wight, including his godson among the Tennyson children:

> For, being of that honest few
> Who give the Fiend himself his due,
>   Should eighty thousand college-councils
> Thunder 'Anathema', friend, at you,
>
> Should all our churchmen foam in spite
> At you, so careful of the right,
>   Yet one lay-hearth would give you welcome –
> Take it and come – to the Isle of Wight. (lines 5–12)[69]

For all the jocular tone, the crisis in Maurice's career was a serious one. The ability of some lay Anglicans even in the relatively doctrinaire climate of the mid-nineteenth-century Church of England to take the official business of the church lightly has much to do with what Anglicanism means for most people today in the Western world.

If grace always implies surprise, then living by grace means living in a way that accords primacy to that surprise and what one has learned from it. The surprise of presence allows us to acknowledge our own human limitations, both our weaknesses that take the form of sin and the constraints upon us as finite creatures – constraints that will eventually take the form of our death. Much of our life we may spend in a state of absence rather than presence. And the poetic tradition offers no remedy for that as such, no mechanisms for bringing it to an end, no particular coping skills. It merely reminds us that it is part of a larger reality that also includes the experience of presence, coming to us without warning and working its transformations on us in ways that we could not have predicted. To live by this grace means living lives entirely human – incarnate in the flesh, connected with the whole complexity that is human community, indeed with a community that stretches beyond the human to the world of nature to which we belong by our creation. In living such a life, most of the poets have at least found the living Christian tradition of Anglicanism helpful. Most have felt that they must sit somewhat lightly to it, accepting whatever seems to explain their encounter with grace and letting some other matters slide into oblivion. Some have felt that they must break with it altogether; yet, they have not always therefore ceased to contribute to the poetic tradition of Anglican spirituality.

5. A LIVING TRADITION

I have described the poetic tradition of Anglican spirituality primarily in terms of its continuities. Every tradition, however, lives in a tension between continuity and change. The continuities I have called attention to are perennial features of the tradition. But, even as I have sought to describe them, I have had to note that the tradition is in constant motion, responding to the changing realities and expectations of every era, expressing its concerns and insights in language intelligible to an audience that does not and cannot stand culturally still. Part of the nature of any living tradition is that it changes and keeps finding a new voice – or, more precisely, new voices. An adequate exploration of this history of change would be a vast undertaking – probably beyond the present author's capacity and certainly beyond this book's. Yet, it is at least necessary to sketch some of the major elements that give the different ages of this tradition their particular, distinctive qualities.

ORIGINS

The poetic tradition of Anglican spirituality came to birth with John Donne and George Herbert under specific and significant historical circumstances.[1] It was the era in which English lyric poetry turned from being an art form predominantly spoken or sung to one predominantly written, printed and read, which also turned out to be a period of explosive creativity in English literature. It was also a period of rare 'normalcy' in the Church of England, which began, in the reigns of Elizabeth I and James I, to assume a concrete, home-grown shape. Only at this point did it, at last, have a period of stability long enough to allow a second generation to reach adulthood in it and take it for granted.[2] Yet it was a period of quiet between storms – the storms of the Reformation itself and of the religious wars of the mid-seventeenth century. Even then it was clear to observant persons that the world was in a protracted crisis of conscience.

However quiet England may have been at the moment, this was an era of competing theologies and the stakes could be very high, both in this age and in the age to come. Any persuasive spirituality had to address this reality. Both Herbert and Donne responded to a particular need of the seventeenth century in concentrating on the authenticity of the experience of God's grace. In the maelstrom of conflicting theologies lay the threat not only of eternal damnation but also of having to account for one's faith in this world at the cost of one's life. Mere intellectual persuasion of the truth of your position must have been cold comfort in the Tower. In this context, what could be more valuable than the reassurance that humanity does indeed, by God's grace, have some experience of God's presence and can receive hope not just from the ebb and flow of learned theological argument, but from one's own discovery of grace? Better yet, if one could not merely read such a message, but be invited to experience it in the analogue of the poem and so be reminded that you had experienced it in your own life.

We should not underestimate the role of individual poets in bringing this poetic tradition to birth and shaping it in decisive ways. Donne and Herbert, as they responded to the spiritual need of their time, were as much the creators of the Anglican ethos as was Cranmer or Hooker or the Virgin Queen. To be sure, they had forerunners. Edmund Spenser, in his *Amoretti*, had already combined the themes of sacred and profane love. On the whole, the poems appeal to the 'profane' Greco-Roman imagery of love, not the Christian.[3] But the poet also begins to understand his love for the beloved in terms of Christ's redeeming love for humanity. He holds Good Friday and Easter up as models of true love and of hope for the future:

> Most glorious Lord of life, that on this day,
>   didst make thy triumph over death and sin:
>   and having harrow'd hell, didst bring away
>   captivity thence captive us to win:
> This joyous day, dear Lord, with joy begin,
>   and grant that we for whom thou diddest die
>   being with thy dear blood clean wash'd from sin,
>   may live for ever in felicity.
> And that thy love we weighing worthily,
>   may likewise love thee for the same again:
>   and for thy sake that all like dear didst buy,
>   with love may one another entertain.
> So let us love, dear love, like as we ought;
>   love is the lesson which the Lord us taught.
>
> (Sonnet 68)[4]

The seed that Spenser planted Donne brings to full flower with his own combination of intense emotion and a tireless and wide-ranging intellect. Donne is not only passionate in love, but attentive to the emotions and very adept at reporting them, at creating an analogue for the 'feel' of them in his poems. The same engaged curiosity that Donne applies to human love he applies also to the intimacy with God that constitutes spirituality. When Donne looks into his experience of God, he finds that the key element, the one that unlocks the rest, is grace. It is not something supplied by himself, but something given in the very relationship. The relationship with God, then, is not a prize earned by abandoning the world, but the surprising visitation of divine grace that brings our perception of the world into right relation with God:

> Know that all lines which circles do contain,
> For once that they the Center touch, do touch
> Twice on the circumference; and be thou such;
> Double on heaven thy thoughts on earth employed;
> All will not serve; Only who have enjoyed
> The sight of God, in fullness, can think it;

For it is both the object, and the wit.

('The Second Anniversary', 436–42)[5]

God is 'both the object and the wit', both the one known in the intimacy of the spiritual conversation and the ability to know.

Those 'who have enjoyed the sight of God in fullness, can think it'. This is the ultimate assurance the era needed. But one will still have to pray and yearn for it. It is not a possession, but a gift – one we misplace and must ask for again. Faith may tell us we received it, but hope is needed to reassure us that the God who gave once gives always. This hope lies behind the exhilaration that the reader feels at the ending of the first of Donne's 'Holy Sonnets'.[6] The first two quatrains seize the reader with a breathless rush of words, analogous to our human helplessness when we depend entirely on our own powers. The speaker appeals to God's grace in creation, but is in a state close to panic because of his insufficiency:

> Thou hast made me, And shall thy work decay?
> Repair me now, for now mine end doth haste,
> I run to death, and death meets me as fast,
> And all my pleasures are like yesterday;
> I dare not move my dim eyes any way,
> Despair behind, and death before doth cast
> Such terror, and my feeble flesh doth waste
> By sin in it, which it t'wards hell doth weigh;

The next quatrain begins with an affirmation of hope, but once again, human power is insufficient. The foe tempts, and the last line of the quatrain is made slow and heavy by an arrangement of words that contradicts normal word order and by being composed primarily of classical spondees (feet composed of two long syllables):

> Only thou art above, and when towards thee
> By thy leave I can look, I rise again;
> But our old subtle foe so tempteth me,
> That not one hour my self I can sustain;

The final couplet comes as a moment of deliverance, partly because it returns to iambs (an unaccented and typically short syllable followed by an accented one), but also because it affirms God's power to act, to become the wit as well as the object.

> Thy Grace may wing me to prevent his art,
> And thou like Adamant draw mine iron heart.

The last two feet ('draw mine iron heart') are again classical spondees, but now their effect is more ambiguous. 'Mine iron heart' is heavy and, in itself immobile. But, for all that, the effect of the magnet (oddly miscalled 'adamant') is irresistible; the movement is slow but inevitable.

Donne gave to the emergent tradition of Anglican poetics a certain psychological realism, a willingness to look directly at our complex emotional and intellectual lives without reducing them to mere principles or theory, an insistence on our need for God's grace and its power to produce hope and connection where we could not produce it for ourselves. Donne had a strong comprehension of how deep a need this is. He seems to have sensed how much darkness is possible in the human soul as well as how much delight we can encompass. His works are imbued with what might easily become desperation were it not for the hope that grace can still give us wings to escape death and loss and alienation from all that we love. He does not back away from the emotional lability of our encounter with God. He touched on the darker side of the spiritual meeting, on its revelation of human weakness, but the grace of God is still there as ultimate presupposition and as precious if rare experience.[7]

George Herbert gave the tradition its milder, more optimistic side – not optimistic about humanity's own powers, but about the ultimate triumph of God's grace in the distressed human spirit. Herbert is as astute as Donne in tracing the complexities and difficulties of the human encounter with God in spirituality, and he is equally immersed in the reality of human emotion. He is more generous, however, in acknowledging and modelling the moments of intimacy granted and enjoyed: 'So I did sit and eat'. The movement toward this consent to grace, however, is neither direct nor easy. Nor is it sufficiently predictable that Herbert can offer a road map. What he offers instead is a series of vignettes along the road, vignettes that may reassure the readers that we have not strayed completely off track, that the grace of God is still alive in us. This is not to say that Herbert regards the spiritual journey as completely unpredictable. It is connected with the life of the Christian community, as the title and form of the collection indicate.[8] Still, the moment of consummation is not found simply in the external rites of the church, but in the innermost and most hidden consciousness of the speaker where 'Love bade me welcome . . .'[9]

As a good parish clergyman, Herbert is interested in the externals of Christian life, too, and encourages a high level of public decency and responsibility. 'The Church Porch' sums this appeal up in an address to the young male, urging such virtues as sexual restraint, temperance and moderation. The goal, however, is not heroic virtue, but common maturity:

Do all things like a man, not sneakingly. (line 121)

Like the wisdom traditions in Proverbs and Ecclesiasticus, Herbert even gives advice about table manners and control of expenses. Dress with 'cheap handsomeness', he advises. 'Be sweet to all.' Do not pick quarrels. Do not laugh too much. And so on at considerable length. The advice is, on the whole, moderate and sensible, much of it still apropos. Still, all this is preliminary. The real goal is not even for the addressee to participate in the life of the church, though Herbert insists on it, but rather what can arise out of worship, the worshipper's spiritual engagement with God. Herbert essays the challenge of drawing back the veil that covers the inner life.[10]

While it is possible to describe Herbert (and virtually all contemporary Anglicans) as Calvinists,[11] the tag misses the point of his spirituality. Even if he endorsed the doctrine of double predestination,[12] his constant endeavour is to reassure his audience of God's gracious goodness as something on which we can place our reliance. Herbert saw the goal of spirituality as a breaking down of barriers. So, for example, the first of the poems called 'Prayer':[13]

> Prayer the Church's banquet, Angels' age,
>   God's breath in man returning to his birth,
>   The soul in paraphrase, heart in pilgrimage,
> The Christian plummet sounding heaven and earth;
>
> Engine against th'Almighty, sinners' tower,
>   Reversèd thunder, Christ-side-piercing spear,
>   The six-days world transposing in an hour,
> A kind of tune, which all things hear and fear;
>
> Softness, and peace, and joy, and love, and bliss,
>   Exalted Manna, gladness of the best,
>   Heaven in ordinary, man well drest,
> The milky way, the bird of Paradise,
>
>   Church-bells beyond the stars heard, the soul's blood,
>   The land of spices; something understood.

At first reading, the poem appears to be a random jumble of appositions, albeit a beautiful and moving one. On further consideration, one discovers that the appositions move back and forth between heaven and earth, between the external and the internal, the temporal and the eternal, the powerful and the gentle. The last line, with its 'land of spices,' alludes to the Song of Solomon's passionate lovers. In that context, the 'something understood' points to their particular intimacy, the 'something understood' available to lovers alone in their mutual absorption and impossible to explain, to make understood in other terms. The poem cannot convey it, only point to it.[14]

When all is said and done, humanity cannot compel this consummation. What we can do is seek it, pray for it, summon it, desire it, lament its absence, and trust that grace will eventually take up residence in our hearts in ways that we will understand only then – the elusive but profoundly real 'something understood'. This vision of a gracious intimacy between

God and humanity is Herbert's particular gift to the Anglican poetic tradition.[15]

THE LATER SEVENTEENTH CENTURY

The successors of Donne and Herbert lived in a radically different world, characterised by the upheavals of the Civil War and the disestablishment of the religion that had nourished them. Under the Commonwealth, the bishops and those clergy sympathetic to them were deprived of office, lay leaders were, in many cases, punished because of their political and religious sympathies, the Book of Common Prayer was prohibited in public worship, and those who remained loyal to the church order familiar from the days of Elizabeth, James and Charles found themselves a powerless and even oppressed population. What had once been merely normal was now, by the turn of political events, forbidden. It was a strange transition, psychologically and spiritually.

Robert Herrick was a clergyman and a royalist. He wrote most of his poetry while a vicar in Devon, a position from which he was expelled in 1647. He published his volume of poetry in 1648, when the royalist cause was clearly lost, and apparently wrote no more.[16] One might read the collection as a kind of reassertion of conservative royalist values in the face of Puritan domination.[17] Certainly, Herrick is master of one feature of the tradition that was critical in the conflict with Puritanism – its apparent frivolity. Herrick refuses to dichotomise, to divide the world neatly into sacred and profane, good and bad. His *Hesperides* are thoroughly incarnational, mixing the fleshly and the spiritual, the erotic and the devout.

Hesperides opens with 'The Argument of his Book',[18] which actually lists the subject matter of many of the poems. It begins with the lightest and brightest images of love poetry and seems at first to categorise the collection as light and profane:[19]

> I sing of brooks, of blossoms, birds and bowers:
> Of April, May, of June, and July-flowers.

> I sing of maypoles, hock-carts, wassails, wakes,
> Of bridegrooms, brides, and of their bridal cakes.
> I write of youth, of love, and have access
> By these to sing of cleanly-wantonness. (lines 1–6)

The odd coinage 'cleanly-wantonness' foreshadows a characteristic claim of Herrick's poetry: that the carnal, fleshly blessings of human existence are not opposed to one's relationship with God, but may indeed form a part of it. Yet there follows a shift to religious topics, concluding with heaven, on which the poet makes a special claim:

> I write of hell; I sing (and ever shall)
> Of heaven, and hope to have it after all. (lines 13–14)

The modern reader may think of this religious reference as merely conventional, but in fact it embodies Herrick's repeated insistence on mixing all kinds of matter together. In this case, Herrick dismisses hell (so fascinating to the religious mind of his time) rather briefly and focuses rather on heaven, something that he sees as more truly characterising the ways of God with humanity.

To Herrick, divine grace is not limited to the 'things of the spirit', but is incarnate in quite earthly things – the ordinary human delights that are equally evidence of God's goodness and care:

> 'Tis thou that crownest my glittering hearth
>   With guiltless mirth,
> And givest me wassail bowls to drink,
>   Spiced to the brink.[20]

These very pleasures lead the soul back toward God in thanksgiving. This human response, however, earns nothing – cannot even compel God's attention. God receives it out of God's own grace, as a voluntary consent to remain in relation with the beloved creature, humanity:

> All these and better thou dost send
>   Me, to this end:

That I should render, for my part,
　　A thankful heart,
Which, fired with incense, I resign
　　As wholly thine;
But the acceptance – that must be,
　　My Christ, by thee. (lines 51–8)

Herrick seems to have an enduring confidence in that acceptance.

Henry Vaughan was less fortunate than Herrick in his times, writing as he did in the depths of the Commonwealth. Vaughan has difficulty, at times, finding his God in the eclipse of his church. Absent that church, the poet can only retreat into the interiority of spirituality to meet God. In 'Jacob's Pillow, and Pillar',[21] which builds on the story of Jacob's dream in Genesis 28, he goes so far as to treat all public religion as suspect and only that of the individual heart as pure. He addresses Jacob as a fellow initiate in this matter, whose commemorative pillar at Bethel held all the access to God anyone could need:

I see the Temple in thy Pillar reared,
And that dread glory, which thy children feared,
In mild, clear visions, without a frown,
Unto thy solitary self is shown.
'Tis number makes a schism: throngs are rude,
And God himself died by the multitude.
This made him put on clouds, and fire and smoke,
Hence he in thunder to thy off-spring spoke;
The small, still voice, at some low cottage knocks,
But a strong wind must break thy lofty rocks. (lines 1–10)

Vaughan describes the religion of the spirit as the Land of Goshen, where the Israelites lived in Egypt and which still enjoyed light when the rest of that land was plagued with darkness (Exodus 10:21–3). It is the church of God at Pergamum, residing at Satan's seat and threatened with martyrdom, but promised salvation (Revelation 2:12–17). If for the moment it must suffer, the faithful can only await God's mercy.

This was the only way Vaughan could find for his faith to continue; but the price was high. In the absence of a living community, he was dependent on a community of the departed, whom he addressed in some of his most memorable writing, for example 'They are all gone into the world of light':[22]

> They are all gone into the world of light!
> 　And I alone sit ling'ring here;
> Their very memory is fair and bright,
> 　And my sad thoughts doth clear. (lines 1–4)

The clearing of his sad thoughts holds out a certain hope, but with increased clarity comes an aching longing for what is absent, a longing that becomes an eagerness to join the departed beloved:

> I see them walking in an air of glory,
> 　Whose light doth trample on my days:
> My days, which are at best but dull and hoary,
> 　Mere glimmerings and decays.
> 　. . .
> Father of eternal life, and all
> 　Created glories under thee!
> Resume thy spirit from this world of thrall
> 　Into true liberty.
>
> Either disperse these mists, which blot and fill
> 　My perspective (still) as they pass,
> Or else remove me hence unto that hill,
> 　Where I shall need no glass. (lines 9–12, 33–40)

Such loneliness stimulated an extraordinarily vivid vision of the hope of the Age to Come, but it was a strange context for continuing a spiritual tradition as profoundly public and communal as the one founded by Donne and Herbert.

Vaughan is left with an abiding sense of distance from God, as if he has been thrown into a kind of exile. He longs for a sense of nearness to replace it, but he can look for it only in the intimacy of the interior life. Full of people as his life was, he longed to be at least an interior anchorite and found himself most alive in the contemplative hours of the night and early morning, as the speaker in 'The Night' suggests:[23]

> Dear night! this world's defeat;
> The stop to busy fools; care's check and curb;
> The day of Spirits, my soul's calm retreat
>   Which none disturb!
> *Christ's* progress, and his prayer time;
> The hours to which high Heaven doth chime.

(lines 25–30)

But perhaps the perfect nearness is possible only beyond death:

> There is in God (some say)
> A deep, but dazzling darkness; as men here
> Say it is late and dusky, because they
>   See not all clear;
> O for that night! where I in him
> Might live invisible and dim. (lines 49–54)

This kind of mystical certainty may have been rare in Vaughan's life, certainly more rare than he wished. But, in some measure, it satisfied the loneliness of his very un-Anglican Anglican existence. 'The Favour'[24] seems to capture something of it:

> O thy bright looks! thy glance of love
> Shown, & but shown me from above!
> Rare looks! that can dispense such joy
> As without wooing wins the coy.
> And makes him mourn, and pine and die
> Like a starved eaglet, for thine eye.
> Some kind herbs here, though low and far,
> Watch for, and know their loving star.
> O let no star compare with thee!
> Nor any herb out-duty me!

So shall my nights and mornings be
Thy time to shine, and mine to see.

The work of prayer and of the Christian life is not a way of earning God's grace, but the one possible response to it. Drawing on herbal lore, Vaughan takes as his example medicinal plants thought to respond to astral influences, suggesting that his life will always have to seek that too fleeting influence of light, once shown from above. Living in a desolate era, he did not find that this attentive hope relieved all his suffering, but it kept him focused on the grace of God past and future. However difficult his life-experience, he is the key figure in bringing the tradition founded by Donne and Herbert over into a world where Anglicanism was no longer the inevitable fact it had seemed to his predecessors.[25]

Thomas Traherne, the last seventeenth-century writer I shall instance here, lived his productive life at the turn from Commonwealth to Restoration, when that moment of transition could still seem like a return to the older Anglicanism. To be sure, no return to the old was truly possible. Its sheer de facto quality was for ever lost. Moreover, the long period out of power had encouraged a tendency to ideologise Anglicanism, a process already begun in Laud's high churchmanship before the Civil War. While Anglicanism still resisted the thoroughgoing kind of theological uniformity that characterised other Western forms of Christianity, it could not return to its older, more simple identification with the nation. Indeed, it grew more and more suspicious of the nation's religious vitality, fearful that every form of enthusiasm might fuel a new war and retreating into the shell of the rational and predictable.

The experience of people like Henry Vaughan, however, during the Commonwealth had changed the relationship between the church and its poetic tradition. Where Vaughan's major predecessors were all clergymen (Donne, Herbert, Herrick), few of his successors would be; and the poetic tradition of spirituality, while not for the most part rejecting the public life of the church and its common prayer, would never be anchored there again in the way it was for Herbert.

Thomas Traherne, clergyman though he was, stands closer, as an exemplar of the poetic spirituality, to Vaughan than to Herbert. He did not lack a pastoral concern for the meaning of Christian life and community, as his *Christian Ethics* shows. But his turn toward childhood as the moment of closest human intimacy with the divine leaves him more focused on the individual element in spirituality than the communal one. He is capable of writing as if nothing else were truly important:

> A quiet silent person may possess
> All that is great or high in blessedness.
> The inward work is the supreme: for all
> The other were occasion'd by the Fall.
> A man, that seemeth idle to the view
> Of others, may the greatest business do.
> Those acts which Adam in his innocence
> Performed, carry all the excellence.
> These outward busy acts he knew not, were
> But meaner matters, of a lower sphere.
> Building of churches, giving to the poor,
> In dust and ashes lying on the floor,
> Adminst'ring of justice, preaching peace,
> Ploughing and toiling for a forc'd increase,
> With visiting the sick, or governing
> The rude and ignorant: this was a thing
> As then unknown.

('Silence', lines 1–17)[26]

Even the most charitable works of religion, much as Traherne would affirm their importance in the fallen world, pale in comparison with the original business of humanity – to know and enjoy God. And this is something that can be known only within:

> That temple David did intend,
> Was but a thought, and yet it did transcend
> King Solomon's. A thought we know

> Is that for which
> God doth enrich
> With joys even Heaven above, and earth below.
>
> ('Thoughts II', lines 25–30)[27]

This emphasis on interiority does not mean that Traherne ignores the reality or the importance of the human community. His vision of the perfect human life is strongly social. He presents a kind of child's-eye view of true human existence in the poem 'Christendom':[28]

> Beneath the lofty trees
> I saw, of all degrees,
> Folk calmly sitting in their doors; while some
> Did standing with them kindly talk,
> Some smile, some sing, or what was done
> Observe, while others by did walk;
> They view'd the boys
> And girls, their joys,
> The streets adorning with their angel-faces,
> Themselves diverting in those pleasant places.
>
> (lines 71–80)

Traherne also acknowledges the importance of mutual human care in the present, fallen state of the world, which he describes in 'Mankind is sick' as a kind of madness. Those blessedly free of this malady are not free of responsibility to the sick: 'The wise and good like kind physicians are' (line 10).[29]

The most distinctive thing, however, in Traherne's spirituality is the ease with which he connects the grace of creation with that of redemption. While orthodox enough in his religion, his spirituality seems focused less on Jesus than on the creation, both the creation of the world and that of the individual. His short poem 'The Bible'[30] is a good example of this shift:

> That! That! There I was told
> That I the son of God was made,
> His image. O divine! And that fine gold,
> With all the joys that here do fade,

Are but a toy, compared to the bliss
Which heavenly, Godlike, and eternal is.

That we on earth are kings;
And, though we're cloth'd with mortal skin,
Are inward cherubins; have angels' wings;
Affections, thoughts, and minds within,
Can soar through all the coasts of Heaven and earth;
And shall be sated with celestial mirth.

As mentioned above, for Traherne, childhood is the moment when we are closest to God. Once we are corrupted by the ways of the world, we make our way back to its purity of vision only slowly and with difficulty.

The point of Traherne's interiority is not quietude, but the delight of the soul's intimacy with God, which is, at the same time, delight in everything that God has made. One of the poems from *Christian Ethics* captures this in the way that it sets contentment aside as too low a goal:

Contentment is a sleepy thing!
If it in death alone must die,
A quiet mind is worse than poverty!
Unless it from enjoyment spring!
That's blessedness alone that makes a king!
Wherein the joys and treasures are so great,
They all the powers of the soul employ,
And fill it with a work complete.

('Contentment is a sleepy thing', lines 1–11)[31]

While this delight is focused in God, Traherne rejects the notion that the soul must somehow be abstracted from the world of which it is a part in order to arrive at the true enjoyment of God. Quite the contrary, he insists:

Wouldst thou love God alone? God alone cannot be beloved. He cannot be loved with a finite love, because He is infinite. Were He beloved alone, His love would be limited. He must be loved in all with an illimited love, even in all His doings,

in all His friends, in all His creatures. Everywhere in all
things thou must meet His love. And this the Law of Nature
commands. And it is thy glory that thou art fitted for it. His
love unto thee is the law and measure of thine unto Him:
His love unto all others the law and obligation of thine unto
all. (*Centuries* 1.72)[32]

Since little of Traherne's work was published in his own time
and the surviving manuscript materials have become available
only in the last century or so, Traherne did not contribute
directly to the developing tradition of Anglican spiritual poetics.
Yet, he was deeply a part of it, as the resurgence of his favourite
theme of childhood a century later in Blake and Wordsworth
shows. He remains the incomparable voice of spiritual delight
in the tradition, but his emphasis on the continuity of all true
delight and love, his emphasis on creation and embodiment,
capture elements vital to the tradition as a whole.

The seventeenth-century poets after Donne and Herbert were
writing in and for a different world – one where Anglicanism
was increasingly defined in opposition to Puritanism, where it
even disappeared for a time as the kind of 'fact on the ground'
it had been for Donne and Herbert, one where it finally became
a denominational choice, albeit the established favourite. The
result was to make the poetic tradition more independent of the
institutional church. The Anglicanism of people like Vaughan
became, in some degree, a kind of private devotion. Even after
the Restoration, the poetry of Traherne makes little assumption
of normal church life. It is highly scriptural, and it contains
references to public worship, to major feasts, to church bells
and buildings. Yet the interior life is of such overwhelming
importance for Traherne that the external elements of religion
weigh relatively less. If one had only the poems to go by, I am
not sure that one would know Traherne was ordained. In this
respect, he is closer to Vaughan and to his successors in later
eras than to Donne or Herbert.

THE EIGHTEENTH CENTURY

After the Restoration, England longed for stability and reasonableness. In the world of poetry, a sea change separated the seventeenth century from the eighteenth. Prosody became more polished and regular, the 'metaphysical' tropes of the seventeenth century were abandoned and ultimately despised, and the subject matter of poetry turned resolutely away from the interior world inhabited by such poets as Vaughan and Traherne toward the wit and rationality of Pope. To be sure, the eighteenth century was very interested in the passions, the temperaments, the mechanics of the human psyche. But, in comparison with the earlier poetry, it was an interest from the outside, part of the new scientific, objectivising approach to the world. It seems observed more than it seems lived in.[33]

Perhaps Traherne's work was already out of keeping with his time – too warm, too 'enthusiastic' for the new temper. More to the current taste was the poetry of Bishop Thomas Ken, still close, metrically, to that of his predecessors, but retaining little of their spark of inner authenticity. His *Christian Year*, with its associated (and still popular) morning and evening hymns,[34] is generally conventional, content to moralise the propers of the day in a kindly and gentle way. At times, he creates a charming verse, but the reader should not expect any shock of spiritual recognition, any surprise of grace. For Ken, spirituality is more or less identical with religion – a known quantity, which merely needs people who will live it out with courage and precision, as he himself did in refusing to break his oath of loyalty to James II by swearing a new one to William and Mary.[35]

If one can speak of a distinctively eighteenth-century spirituality, it was focused on evenness and moderation; and it appears most clearly in the realm of music rather than poetry. Charles Jennens[36] expressed it (albeit in mediocre poetry) in his libretto for Handel's oratorio *L'Allegro, il Penseroso ed il Moderato*. The main part of the libretto is a dialogue between the melancholy and sanguine temperaments, which Jennens created by a skilful pastiche of Milton's poems 'L'Allegro' and 'Il Penseroso'.[37] But

Jennens added an up-to-date conclusion, 'Il Moderato', in which he exhorts the audience to abandon the extremes of both mirth and melancholy:

> Keep as of old, the middle way,
> Nor deeply sad, nor idly gay
> But still the same in look and gait,
> Easy, cheerful and sedate. (lines 9–12)

His ideal is

> . . . contentment true,
> Whom headlong passion never knew. (lines 15–16)

The poem concludes by saluting the rise of a new and less passionate day:

> As steals the morn upon the night,
> And melts the shades away:
> So truth does fancy's charm dissolve,
> The fumes that did the mind involve,
> Restoring intellectual day. (lines 43–7)[38]

Jennens's poetry is pallid. Indeed, one wonders whether his 'contentment' was of precisely that sleepy variety that Traherne found wanting because it springs from avoidance rather than enjoyment.[39] Yet, the ideal thus expressed could evoke real attachment at the time, as becomes clear in Handel's music. Handel set the last lines as a duet, with music that both recalls the contrasting passions of the earlier 'debate' and transcends them:

> [T]he mind's dualism sings as one. It is not the victory of Reason but 'the fumes that did the mind involve' which are evoked once more now, hinting at the complex of human passions and desires beneath the controlling surface of the will. This duet is the real culmination of the work . . .[40]

And the music for the words 'intellectual day' is as transcendently beautiful as anything Handel ever wrote, suggesting that such a day signifies far more than barren ratiocination.[41]

William Boyce's oratorio *Solomon,* with a libretto by one Edward Moore based on the Song of Solomon, has a similar movement toward tranquillity, though it remains close to the traditional Christian reading of the Song of Songs. Indeed, the text may be read simply as an erotic pastoral; yet it is transparent enough to its biblical archetype that, even apart from the title of the work, the contemporary audience would have been unable to miss its origins. The work remained popular in performance till about the end of the century, when its eroticism was apparently found too embarrassing for further use.[42]

The art of spirituality, then, may have changed muses and moved to the concert hall. But it did not completely abandon the poetic field. Thomas Gray found a complex, but successful way to bring the subject matter of spiritual interiority back into poetry in his *Elegy Written in a Country Church-Yard.*[43] He focuses the reader's attention on an anonymous village youth who might, under other circumstances, have been a poet – or, for there is ambiguity here, may be the poet himself, reconceived as village youth. The poem begins in pastoral mode, thus allowing the reader to break from the associations of contemporary educated, urban life, with its wariness and scepticism about inner depths:

> The Curfew tolls the knell of parting day,
> The lowing herd wind slowly o'er the lea,
> The ploughman homeward plods his weary way,
> And leaves the world to darkness and to me. (lines 1–4)

With the hour and the scene, Gray establishes a world reminiscent of 'Il Penseroso', where a reflective melancholy would be thought at home.

From here the meditation moves to the dead – specifically the poor, who are buried in the churchyard, not in fine monuments within the church. But in death, all are equal, an element expressed ritually in the relative impersonality and lack of individual reference in the funeral liturgy of the Book of Common Prayer. Indeed, these village folk, says Gray, had the same potential as the mightiest, denied full flowering only by their lack of education and opportunity. The poet even suggests that the advantages of the élite are not unmixed, that something more genuinely human as well as simpler might be found among these poor:

> Far from the madding crowd's ignoble strife,
> Their sober wishes never learned to stray;
> Along the cool sequester'd vale of life
> They kept the noiseless tenor of their way. (lines 73–6)

This idealising of the simple life had a long history in both ancient and modern languages. But Gray makes a particular use of it here that pulls it into the realm of spirituality. He draws the audience to focus on a person who both is and is not the speaker of the poem, a 'thee' whom the speaker addresses. It is, in fact, the poet himself, but not officiously claimed as 'I'. In fact, the poet invites the reader to hear his story as told by a third party in the third person:

> For thee, who mindful of th'unhonoured Dead
> Dost in these lines their artless tale relate;
> If chance, by lonely contemplation led
> Some kindred Spirit shall inquire thy fate,
>
> Haply some hoary-headed Swain may say,
> 'Oft have we seen him at the peep of dawn . . .' (lines 93–8)

In this way, the figure of the speaker is made sufficiently uncertain – an 'I', a 'thee', a 'him' – that it could be anyone, even the reader. And when the reader is at length invited to peruse the poet's epitaph – 'Approach and read (for thou canst read)' – it could prove to be the reader's epitaph, too.

Gray accepts the common eighteenth-century identification of the contemplative and poetic person as melancholic:

> Here rests his head upon the lap of Earth
> A Youth to Fortune and to Fame unknown,
> Fair Science frown'd not on his humble birth,
> And Melancholy mark'd him for her own. (lines 117–20)

But the poet goes on to assert the possibilities inherent in such a temperament:

> Large was his bounty, and his soul sincere,
> Heav'n did a recompense as largely send:
> He gave to Mis'ry all he had, a tear,
> He gain'd from Heav'n ('twas all he wish'd) a friend.
>
> No farther seek his merits to disclose,
> Or draw his frailties from their dread abode,
> (There they alike in trembling hope repose,)
> The bosom of his Father and his God. (lines 121–8)

The intimacy of friendship with God proves to be a sufficient consummation in the absence of worldly success. This intimacy with God is not an externally measurable religious and moral attainment; the poet continues to be a person of frailties as well as merits, both alike hidden with him in God's bosom. This friendship belongs rather to the inwardness of spirituality.[44]

For much of the eighteenth century, the primary poetic expression of spirituality took the form of hymns, many of which show real poetic excellence. The public nature of hymns, however, and the expectation that they would reinforce the presuppositions and expectations of the groups that sang them necessarily affected the interaction of 'reader' and text.[45] We have mentioned above the work of Christopher Smart, whose poetry is hymnlike in its more formal mode (the 'Hymn to David') and psalmlike in its more erratic ones ('Jubilate Agno'). A more typical author, however, is Charles Wesley, a priest of the Church of England who was deeply involved in the pious and revivalistic movements led by his brother John, but adamantly opposed to any separation of the Methodists from the established church. A great many of his hymns remain in use, a testimony both to the felicity of their language and to the way they engage the singer's spirituality.

The Methodist movement, after all, was not only perfectionist (like much of eighteenth-century Anglican piety) but also concerned to reconnect the emotions with religion. Charles Wesley recommended his 1780 collection of hymns 'to every truly pious reader: as a means of raising or quickening the spirit of devotion, of confirming his faith, of enlivening his hope, and of kindling or increasing his love to God and man'.[46] In the hymns themselves, Wesley's language sometimes recalls that of Herbert or Vaughan. One hears, for example, Vaughan's evocations of light in these lines 'Describing Inward Religion':

> Faith lends its realizing light,
>   The clouds disperse, the shadows fly;
> Th'Invisible appears in sight,
>   And God is seen by mortal eye.[47]

And these verses from a communion hymn echo Herbert's 'Love (III)':

> Our hearts we open wide,
>   To make the Saviour room,
> And lo! the Lamb, the Crucified,
>   The sinner's Friend, is come!
>   His presence makes the feast;
>   And now our bosoms feel
> The glory not to be exprest,
>   The joy unspeakable.
>
> With pure celestial bliss
>   He doth our spirits cheer,
> His house of banqueting is this,
>   And he hath brought us here:
>   He doth his servants feed
>   With manna from above,
> His banner over us is spread,
>   His everlasting love.[48]

There are both gains and losses in the transition from lyric poetry to hymn. There is a gain in public accessibility, but a potential loss in interiority. What in Vaughan or Herbert is a hope held alongside the soul's own resistance to it, ultimately to be resolved in the surprise of grace, in the context of public worship may easily become an expectation, something that the pious person works toward, tries to feel, endeavours to achieve – all the while formally acknowledging, of course, that it is dependent on the grace of God.

Charles Wesley's hymnic gift was not isolated. An astonishing trove of distinguished English hymnody dates from the eighteenth century, and much of it celebrates the discovery of grace. John Newton's 'Amazing Grace' is a familiar example. The distinguished poet William Cowper also contributed to Newton's Olney collection of hymns. Cowper, perhaps in part because of his periodic bouts of insanity, was able to write of the uncontrollable and unpredictable nature of grace in a way as compelling as Vaughan. He sometimes takes a more general approach, as in the familiar hymn 'God moves in a mysterious way/His wonders to perform', and sometimes a quite deliberately personal one:

> Sometimes a light surprises
>   The Christian while he sings;
> It is the Lord who rises
>   With healing in his wings:
> When comforts are declining,
>   He grants the soul again
> A season of clear shining,
>   To cheer it after rain.[49]

The hymns of Charles Wesley or William Cowper appear against the background of an overall social consensus that the world was and should remain stable. As Alexander Pope had expressed it for the century as a whole: 'Whatever is is right.'[50] This meant, among other things, that the job of religion was to teach people how to live within the status quo. Increasingly, however, the status quo became unlivable, as revolutions in America and France made clear. By the end of the eighteenth century, issues of spirituality could no longer be detached from public concerns.

REBELLION AND ROMANTICISM

What would Anglican spirituality look like if it began once again, as in Vaughan, to criticise the social world? One form it might and did take was William Blake's *Songs of Innocence* and *Songs of Experience*. In some respects, Blake is very much a part of the tradition we have been tracing. In other ways, he represents a sharp break.[51] He has little good to say of the church and much bad. Yet he criticises the church, as we have seen, in the name of the gospel itself. In Blake, perhaps for the first time, we see a Christian spirituality not merely detached from but fundamentally in opposition to Christian religion as it existed then.[52]

Still, Blake's emphasis on childhood and its nearness to divinity places him in the tradition of Vaughan's 'The Retreat'. Blake celebrates childhood divinity with as much confidence as his predecessor in 'Infant Joy'[53] (from *Songs of Innocence*):

> 'I have no name:
> I am but two days old.'
> What shall I call thee?
> 'I happy am,
> Joy is my name.'
> Sweet joy befall thee!
>
> Pretty joy!
> Sweet joy but two days old,
> Sweet joy I call thee:
> Thou dost smile,
> I sing the while
> Sweet joy befall thee.

But there is also another side to the matter for Blake. Vaughan speaks of sin entering into the infant, learned no doubt from companions and leaving its deep mark in the soul. For Blake, the terrible thing is what the world does *to* the child, not just *in* the child. And the church is part of the world that assaults the innocent. In the first of two poems called 'Holy

Thursday'[54] (found in *Songs of Innocence*), he celebrates a gathering of children to sing in St Paul's Cathedral as a kind of vision of perfect human community. Its counterpart from *Songs of Experience*[55] is bleaker:

> Is this a holy thing to see
> In a rich and fruitful land,
> Babes reduc'd to misery,
> Fed with cold and usurous hand?
>
> Is that trembling cry a song?
> Can it be a song of joy?
> And so many children poor?
> It is a land of poverty! (lines 1–8)

The parallel with the first 'Holy Thursday' poem makes it clear that Blake is condemning the church specifically.

Blake printed his *Songs* in 1794, but his work long remained outside of the mainstream of English poetry. For that mainstream, the turning point came in 1798 with the publication of *Lyrical Ballads* by William Wordsworth and Samuel Taylor Coleridge.[56] Wordsworth turned the poetic tradition in a new direction, emphasising the role of nature in a way that only Traherne (unknown to Wordsworth) had foreshadowed. He also insisted that genuine humanity was most accessible in children, the poor and otherwise marginalised persons. In both respects, Wordsworth might be seen as continuing the initiative of Gray, but where Gray resorted to a fairly complex circumlocution to make his rustic poet acceptable to his readers, Wordsworth plunged straight in. The intense antagonism that long attended his poetry is not surprising; it was thoroughly shocking in its context.

For Wordsworth, the outward gaze toward nature and the human community is combined with an inward one. He wants to return to a directness in dealing with emotion and spirit that the eighteenth century had prohibited. He simply found that the two went together, that he moved inward most readily in the context of the natural world, as in 'Lines composed a few miles above Tintern Abbey . . .':[57]

> I have felt
> A presence that disturbs me with the joy
> Of elevated thoughts; a sense sublime
> Of something far more deeply interfused,
> Whose dwelling is the light of setting suns,
> And the round ocean and the living air,
> And the blue sky, and in the mind of man;
> A motion and a spirit that impels
> All thinking things, all objects of all thought,
> And rolls through all things. Therefore am I still
> A lover of the meadows and the woods
> And mountains . . . (lines 93–104)

'Thinking things' and 'objects of thought' are united by a single motion and spirit, not divided from one another by the dist-ancing, objectivising mode of the Enlightenment.

Wordsworth also had a concern for the social order and its crimes. He saw the political as the spiritual, as in a familiar sonnet:[58]

> The world is too much with us; late and soon,
> Getting and spending, we lay waste our powers:
> Little we see in Nature that is ours;
> We have given our hearts away, a sordid boon!
> The Sea that bares her bosom to the moon;
> The winds that will be howling at all hours,
> And are up-gathered now like sleeping flowers;
> For this, for everything, we are out of tune;
> It moves us not. – Great God! I'd rather be
> A Pagan suckled in a creed outworn;
> So might I, standing on this pleasant lea,
> Have glimpses that would make me less forlorn;
> Have sight of Proteus rising from the sea;
> Or hear old Triton blow his wreathèd horn.

Wordsworth, unlike Blake or the later Romantics, seems to

have felt no need to abandon the Church of England. (Indeed, he wrote three long series of *Ecclesiastical Sonnets* later in life.) But he did not tie himself absolutely to Christian language. He could also express his sense of the Holy in the language of the old paganism or in language that has seemed pantheistic to some. Still, like his predecessors, Wordsworth could actually create in poetry an analogue of the surprise of grace, as in a stanza that is perhaps his most commonly remembered and recognised one:[59]

> I wandered lonely as a cloud
> That floats on high o'er vales and hills,
> When all at once I saw a crowd,
> A host, of golden daffodils;
> Beside the lake, beneath the trees,
> Fluttering and dancing in the breeze. (lines 1–6)

While the lines may seem hackneyed to us because of over-exposure, they have remained popular because they embody the moment of discovery, the moment when grace alters our view of the entire world.

Samuel Taylor Coleridge, like Wordsworth, retained a connection with the church. Indeed, he was a significant theologian in his own right. But like Wordsworth, he is willing to accept the moment of discovery either in purely natural terms or, as in 'Hymn Before Sun-Rise, in the Vale of Chamouni',[60] with reference to the Creator:

> Thou too again, stupendous Mountain! thou
> That as I raise my head, awhile bowed low
> In adoration, upward from thy base
> Slow travelling with dim eyes suffused with tears,
> Solemnly seemest, like a vapoury cloud,
> To rise before me – Rise, O ever rise,
> Rise like a cloud of incense, from the Earth!
> Thou kingly Spirit throned among the hills,
> Thou dread ambassador from Earth to Heaven,
> Great hierarch! tell thou the silent sky,

> And tell the stars, and tell yon rising sun
> Earth, with her thousand voices, praises God.
>
> (lines 74–85)

Perhaps Coleridge's most significant contribution to the tradition was his theory of the imagination, which he distinguishes sharply from mere fancy. Fancy is 'a mode of memory emancipated from the order of time and space; and blended with, and modified by that empirical phenomenon of the will, which we express by the word choice'. The imagination, however, which lies at the root of true poetry, is, in its primary sense, 'the living power and prime agent of all human perception, and . . . a repetition in the finite mind of the eternal act of creation in the infinite I AM'.[61] Accordingly, Coleridge rejects speech that is either abstract or allegorical (which he regards as merely another mode of the abstract) in favour of the symbolic, which operates 'above all by the translucence of the eternal through and in the temporal. It always partakes of the reality which it renders intelligible.'[62]

In this way, Coleridge offered his successors a conception of poetic speech that made it independent of the rationalism and scientific objectivism increasingly dominating the English language. This conviction emerges from and explains Coleridge's assurance that the poet was in fact a prophet of the Holy:

> Beware! Beware!
> His flashing eyes, his floating hair!
> Weave a circle round him thrice,
> And close your eyes with holy dread,
> For he on honey-dew hath fed,
> And drunk the milk of Paradise.[63]

The eighteenth century was a powerfully formative era for the Anglican poetic tradition. The retreat from spirituality that marked the religious life of the day (to be replaced by duty and the more highly regulated pieties of Methodism and Evangelicalism) and the retreat from interiority that marked its intellectual life (to be replaced by moralism and the objective distancing of the Enlightenment) together formed a barren field for such poetics. Yet, religion and science could not permanently lock the spirit in. It makes its claims again, in varying ways, in Gray, in Blake, in Wordsworth and in Coleridge. It returns, however, in a new form. Gray may situate his *Elegy* in a country church-yard; Wordsworth and Coleridge may remain in communion with the church. But their poetic language is not limited to Christian imagery in the same degree as that of their seventeenth-century predecessors. They use the store of classical imagery brought to new life in the eighteenth century, and they immerse themselves in the world of nature and of ordinary humanity. The spirituality of the Anglican poetic tradition would not again be tied to the religion of the Church of England as tightly as before.

THE VICTORIAN ERA

The situation for our tradition in the early nineteenth century was still difficult. The later Romantics tended to reject Christianity even more absolutely than Blake. And the standard of educated English discourse was increasingly a kind of objective, scientific prose which excluded faith and feeling from consideration. Wordsworth's interest was in nature as experienced, not nature as objectified and made subject first to scientific analysis and then to technological control – the nature that rapidly became central to Victorian culture. Still, the early Romantics had opened a way. John Keble was a great admirer of Wordsworth,[64] and, reading his extremely popular hymns, one can understand why. Wordsworth gave him the language to reconnect Christian spirituality to daily experience:

> Old friends, old scenes, will lovelier be,
> As more of Heaven in each we see;
> Some softening gleam of love and prayer
> Shall dawn on every cross and care.
>
> ('Morning', lines 32–6)[65]

The sentiments owe something to Herbert, too; but they have

about them the attention to humble domesticity of which Wordsworth was the new master.[66]

The great challenge continued to be that of finding or creating a mode of discourse that could speak convincingly about spirituality. Wordsworth had turned to the poor and to nature and Coleridge to the highly imaginative. How was one to speak now to the spiritual possibilities of an emerging middle class, educated in the presuppositions of science and increasingly defined by the bewildering pace of technological change? Perhaps the single most decisive poetic response to this challenge was Tennyson's *In Memoriam*. Like much of Wordsworth, it moves in the realm of the private and domestic, focusing on Tennyson's grief at the death of his friend and exploring the development and maturing of that grief. Tennyson, however, was not one of the 'humble poor', who could be divorced from the larger intellectual life of the time. He was the son of a clergyman and well educated. He finds himself struggling, then, not only with his emotions and the social expectations attached to grief in the period,[67] but also with contemporary developments in the natural sciences, particularly geology (Lyell's work) and palaeontology (the first dinosaur fossils). Many of the challenges that would confront the church more overtly in Charles Darwin's *Origin of Species* a few years later were already implicit in intellectual developments as Tennyson wrote. And Tennyson was sensitive to their meaning. They portrayed a nature very different from that of Wordsworth – a world of struggle and instability, a world in which God appeared irrelevant, the kind of world implied, if not necessarily demanded, by the scientific method.

In the long run, Tennyson deals with the challenge of scientific thought and language neither on its own terms nor by denying its validity, but by asserting that it is an incomplete representation of human reality. The evidence of the new geology is inescapable, but the accompanying reductionism is not:

There rolls the deep where grew the tree.
  O earth, what changes hast thou seen!
  There where the long street roars, hath been
The stillness of the central sea.

The hills are shadows, and they flow
  From form to form, and nothing stands;
  They melt like mist, the solid lands,
Like clouds they shape themselves and go.

But in my spirit will I dwell,
  And dream my dream, and hold it true;
  For tho' my lips may breathe adieu,
I cannot think the thing farewell. (cxxiii)[68]

The spirit is another side of human experience as inescapable as the objectivities of science, even though it is difficult to maintain one's grip on it, one's confidence in it:

If e'er when faith had fall'n asleep,
  I heard a voice 'believe no more,'
  And heard an ever breaking shore
That tumbled in the Godless deep;

A warmth within the breast would melt
  The freezing reason's colder part,
  And like a man in wrath the heart
Stood up and answer'd 'I have felt.'

No, like a child in doubt and fear;
  But that blind clamour made me wise . . .

(cxxiv, lines 9–18)[69]

Again, the scientific doubt is not so much rejected as counterbalanced by the insistence on the significance of emotional and/or spiritual experience. Far from being a lessening of human understanding, Tennyson asserts, this is an enlargement of it; it serves to make one wise.

Tennyson holds a great many things in tension in *In Memoriam* – a fact both demanded and explained by his subject matter, for grief does not move steadily or in a single direction and does not reach a simple resolution so much as it finds a delicate, livable balance. The poems return repeatedly to the same issues without ever resolving them. While he can speak of nature, in terms of the new sciences, as 'red in tooth and claw' (lvi, line 11),[70] he can also seek solace in a Wordsworthian sense of communion with nature and, through nature, with the deceased Hallam, whose 'voice is on the rolling air' and who pervades the natural world for him (cxxx).[71]

This willingness to live with unresolved tensions enables Tennyson to affirm the value of uncertainty and doubt for the spiritual life:

> There lives more faith in honest doubt,
> Believe me, than in half the creeds. (xcvi, lines 11–12)[72]

The point is not to suggest that doubt is better than faith, but rather that the spiritual journey cannot take place without it.[73] Indeed, it is faith in some coherence beyond our human guessing, that makes it possible to doubt:

> Whatever I have said or sung,
>   Some bitter notes my harp would give,
>   Yea, tho' there often seemed to live
> A contradiction on the tongue,
>
> Yet Hope had never lost her youth;
>   She did but look through dimmer eyes:
>   Or Love but play'd with gracious lies,
> Because he felt so fix'd in truth . . . (cxxv, lines 1–8)[74]

What Tennyson found for himself and authorised for his readers was the power to live with loss in a growing confidence that it would not destroy him. The point, after all, is not to affirm the doctrines of creeds, but to remain in communion with God and with those one loves.

The soul seeks the communion of God and of departed friends because it *must*, cries out because it has *felt*. And even the outcry serves to make it wise, by bringing its attention to rest in

Love. Tennyson does not invoke a quick and easy transformation of the emotions, but rather the difficult process of living
attentively with the reality of grief, through which he finds a
renewed discovery of grace, such as was quite beyond any possible expectation in the beginning. He admits that much in this
crisis of grief and faith simply could not be worked out on the
level of everyday rationality.

The role of emotion in Tennyson and other nineteenth-
century poets is sometimes problematic for modern readers.
Because the emotion of the Victorians has often struck twentieth-century readers as overblown and sentimental, we are
inclined to miss what a challenge it was to introduce intense
emotions of doubt and grief into the poetic repertoire after the
eighteenth century. Even among the Romantics, these emotions,
while allowed, were less welcome than the more modified,
reflected emotions of loss, regret, or nostalgia prominent in
Keats or the heroic moods of ardour and idealism favoured by
Shelley or Byron. Tennyson exposes his inner life in astonishing
ways in *In Memoriam*. The speaker admits that friends disap-
proved of the length and overtness of his grief. He describes his
grief over Hallam with images drawn from the socially more
accepted grief of the married – the ongoing grief of a widower,
the loss of a fiancé as felt by his intended bride, and so forth.
The surprising number of female images may be related to the
fact that grief – indeed most sorts of intense emotion – was
the prerogative of Victorian women more than men.

Like Tennyson, Elizabeth Barrett Browning is sometimes
emotionally direct in a way that awakens discomfort in today's
readers. Part of the difficulty is that she is known to most of
us, if at all, only through extracts from her *Sonnets from the
Portuguese* – the bonbons, as it were, of the cycle. Her longer
poems, such as 'Casa Guidi Windows', and her verse novel
Aurora Leigh, create a very different impression with their
clear-eyed reflections on the ideals and politics of the Risorgi-
mento and on the social shortcomings of the Victorian industrial
economy in England. The *Sonnets from the Portuguese* themselves read very differently when one reads them entire. They

are an often painful, but also quite revelatory account of a talented Victorian woman's difficult path toward appropriate self-regard – a process both assisted and rendered more difficult by love for a man.

In an era when social definitions of gender were a subject of great tension and distress, Barrett Browning brings a female voice back into the poetics of English spirituality – a voice largely suppressed since the time of Julian of Norwich. In 'The Virgin Mary to the Child Jesus',[75] Barrett Browning employed her extraordinarily supple prosody, close to spoken English, yet poetically flexible, in reworking the traditional themes of incarnation from a specifically female perspective. Speaking through Mary, she sums up, for example, the experience of inadequacy in the presence of the divine that is a long-standing part of the poetic tradition we are treating here:

> For me – for me –
> God knows that I am feeble like the rest! –
> I often wandered forth, more child than maiden,
> Among the midnight hills of Galilee,
>   Whose summits looked heaven-laden;
> Listening to silence as it seemed to be
> God's voice, so soft yet strong – so fain to press
> Upon my heart as Heaven did on the height,
> And waken up its shadows by a light,
> And show its vileness by a holiness.
> Then I knelt down most silent like the night,
>   Too self-renounced for fears . . . (vii, lines 1–12)

The stanza reflects the penitential quality common to the Anglican poetic tradition.[76] Equally representative, however, is the strongly erotic imagery which hints at the greatest possible intimacy between God and even the sinful soul: the silence of God's voice is 'fain to press/Upon my heart as Heaven did on the height'. The poem is not primarily about penitence, but about a great love that may evoke a sense of insufficiency as a consequence.

Christina Rossetti was less directly emotional than Barrett

Browning. Even when she writes in the first person, she maintains a distance, sometimes deliberately teasing the reader with the impossibility of finding out what is truly in her mind and heart:

> I tell my secret? No indeed, not I:
> Perhaps some day, who knows?
> But not today; it froze, and blows, and snows,
> And you're too curious: fie!
> You want to hear it? well:
> Only, my secret's mine, and I won't tell.
>
> ('Winter: My Secret', lines 1–6)[77]

Rossetti's rhythms and diction, like that of her American contemporary Emily Dickinson, may easily lull the inattentive reader into thinking that there is nothing of much import in her verse, but she was a person insistent on the difficulty of human life and the precariousness of hope. She is often the subversive voice questioning the vaunted confidence (and self-centredness) of Victorian culture.

In ' "To what purpose is this waste" '[78] the speaker, like a good Victorian entrepreneur, deplores nature's tendency to 'waste' its beauty and productivity in places where they cannot benefit humanity. But then she finds herself reproved by a deeper vision granted in a dream:

> All voices of all things inanimate
> Join with the song of angels and the song
> Of blessed Spirits, chiming with
> Their Hallelujahs. One wind wakeneth
> Across the sleeping sea, crisping along
> The waves, and brushes thro' the great
> Forests and tangled hedges, and calls out
> Of rivers a clear sound,
> And makes the ripe corn rustle on the ground,
> And murmurs in a shell;
> Till all their voices swell
> Above the clouds in one loud hymn

Joining the song of Seraphim,
Or like pure incense circle round about
The walls of Heaven, or like a well-spring rise
In shady Paradise. (lines 49–65)[79]

In this way, the truer deeper purpose of nature proves to be revelation and the whole is transparent to God.

Rossetti eschews Victorian optimism. Like Eve, she sees herself as shut out of paradise:

The door was shut. I looked between
    Its iron bars: and saw it lie,
    My garden, mine, beneath the sky,
Pied with all flowers bedewed and green:

From bough to bough the song-birds crossed,
    From flower to flower the moths and bees;
    With all its nests and stately trees
It had been mine, and it was lost.

('Shut Out', lines 1–8)[80]

Rossetti, like Coleridge and Tennyson, also turned to the realm of legend and symbol, her narrative poems often evoking the worlds of ballad or fairy tale. This is not a goal in its own right for her, however. Her greatest and most enduring work, as in 'Goblin Market', uses the imaginative narrative to suggest the possibility of grace breaking through into the closed 'rational' Victorian world. The reductionism implicit in nineteenth-century prose discourse made it increasingly unusable for this purpose. Still, the goal was not to displace the distancing discourse so much as to place another alongside it. As with Tennyson in *In Memoriam*, this poetry can be criticised for not replying more forcibly and intellectually to the scientific issues of the day. But the criticism misses the point, which was not to present an intellectual resolution of academic issues, but to enlarge the language so that it can speak of things that cannot be brought to expression in other kinds of discourse.

The deep need for this sort of move in Victorian culture also comes to light in the work of two other Anglican poets who might not ordinarily be mentioned in the context of spirituality: Edward Lear and Charles Lutwidge Dodgson (Lewis Carroll). I suspect it is no accident that the two supreme masters of non-sense were Victorian Anglicans.[81] Both appreciated the importance of language that did not 'mean' anything in the restricted sense the nineteenth century gave to that word. They staked out an arena that lay outside – or even burst – the reductionist bounds of scientific language. Much of the nonsense of Lewis Carroll's Alice books is a deliberate play on scientific and mathematical presuppositions, while Lear's 'Nonsense Botany' and 'The Jumblies' play on currents in the worlds of natural history. At the same time, their work plays with basic human issues of danger, loss, fear, hope, despair – all in ways sufficiently ridiculous and eccentric that the reader, too, can afford to play. The solemnity and rationality of well-armoured Victorian middle-class life is momentarily dissolved and the larger, more dangerous and unpredictable world allowed in.[82]

The true stature of Dodgson and Lear's achievement is per-ceptible only when one realises how truly rare it is. There is a great deal of topical 'nonsense' in the literature of the last century and a half, but, except for Edith Sitwell's *Façade*, it more commonly belongs to the older mode of Swiftian satire. Part of the rarity of the works of Dodgson and Lear is that they do not often leave a bitter aftertaste. They liberate from the mundane world; they do not drag the reader back into its frays. In doing so, they responded to a deep spiritual thirst for a use of language that is not instrumental, not objective, not analytical, not overtly useful at all but simply partakes in the human talent for presence, for play and for surprise.

Other bearers of the spiritual tradition in the Victorian era do make use of the more objectivising language of the period. They cannot, as a result, offer as direct an account of spiritual experience as Tennyson, Barrett Browning and Rossetti. The approach of Matthew Arnold was rather to acknowledge his world's loss of faith and to identify the personal hollowness that resulted. In a world that no longer had words for spirituality – at least, not ones that the educated were likely to take seriously

– one could only point to the vacuum that loss had left behind it. In a well-known passage from 'Dover Beach',[83] the pulsating roar of the surf evokes this reflection:

> The Sea of Faith
> Was once, too, at the full, and round earth's shore
> Lay like the folds of a bright girdle furl'd.
> But now I only hear
> Its melancholy, long, withdrawing roar,
> Retreating, to the breath
> Of the night-wind, down the vast edges drear
> And naked shingles of the world. (lines 21–8)

This loss of faith brings one into a world of radical fear and uncertainty, where there may be nothing to hang onto except human love:

> Ah, love, let us be true
> To one another! for the world, which seems
> To lie before us like a land of dreams,
> So various, so beautiful, so new,
> Hath really neither joy, nor love, nor light,
> Nor certitude, nor peace, nor help for pain;
> And we are here as on a darkling plain
> Swept with confused alarms of struggle and flight,
> Where ignorant armies clash by night. (lines 29–37)

The modern objectifying and analysing tendency has left the individual spiritually adrift.

One might object that the spirituality evidenced in Arnold's poetry is secularised and unrelated to anything distinctively Christian. In a sense this is true. He himself saw the importance of the Christian tradition primarily in ethical terms.[84] And yet, in this respect, he is speaking the language required by his era, an era excited by the recognition of general laws, not by specific moments of recognition – and particularly wary of 'revealed doctrine'. The astonishing thing is not that his language is generalised, but that he continues to insist on the centrality of the particular as the arena in which grace makes itself known.[85]

The problematic that faced the poets of the Anglican spiritual tradition at the end of the nineteenth century included a number of interrelated challenges posed by the intellectual world in which the poets moved: the 'objectification' of knowledge and language; the subordination of feeling and its relegation to the female sphere, divorced from the 'real' world of men; and suspicion of religious systems as superstitious survivals that impeded the emerging science and technology. The search for a way to express Christian spiritual experience more fully in this milieu necessarily continued until the environment itself began to change, a change that became inescapable in the First World War, then built in intensity over the first half of the twentieth century.

Two poets bridge this gap: Gerard Manley Hopkins and T. S. Eliot. Both are normally thought of as 'moderns' rather than 'Victorians'; but, in terms of their spirituality if not their prosody, they were still working primarily in terms of the Victorian problematic. Hopkins's 'terrible' sonnets express more forcibly the sense of alienation from self and from hope that Arnold also identified in his more urbane way. Eliot, a much cooler, more detached and intellectual poet, is preoccupied with the same theme – as early as 'The Love Song of J. Alfred Prufrock'. For many people, Eliot succeeded in creating a language of faith sufficiently private and allusive that the question of 'objective truth' – of exact one-for-one correspondence between word and thing – no longer arose. The triumph of *The Waste Land* and *Ash Wednesday* was to create a way of speaking about the life of the spirit that connects with the Christian traditions of the West but also uses other ways of conveying religious meaning (e.g., the Tarot), thus suggesting a broader universe of spiritual discourse.[86] Eliot's speech also avoids the impression that it is at all interested in rivalling expository prose at its own game. The sheer incomprehensibility of much of his poetry may act in part as a warning against the conceptualising of what cannot be conceptualised.[87] Eventually, in his late work *The Four Quartets*, Eliot embraces a language honed by ancient Christian mysticism:

To arrive where you are, to get from where you are not,
   You must go by a way wherein there is no ecstasy.
In order to arrive at what you do not know
   You must go by a way which is the way of ignorance.
In order to possess what you do not possess
   You must go by the way of dispossession.
In order to arrive at what you are not
   You must go through the way in which you are not.
And what you do not know is the only thing you know
And what you own is what you do not own
And where you are is where you are not.

               (*East Coker* III, lines 36–46)[88]

This language is about as far from nineteenth-century scientific expository prose as one can get (though it may be less distant from twentieth-century physics). It is closer to the apophatic mysticism of the Dionysian tradition. It is also close to the repeated emphasis of Eliot's Anglican predecessors on the human weakness and inability that can only leave us to wait on the gift of grace. The section from which I have just quoted begins:

O dark dark dark. They all go into the dark,
The vacant interstellar spaces, the vacant into the vacant,
The captains, merchant bankers, eminent men of
letters . . .[89]

It reads not unlike a less optimistic Henry Vaughan, if one can conceive such a person. For the twentieth century it therefore carries an air of integrity.

For facing the twentieth century and its evils head on, however, we need other voices.[90] This is not to criticise Eliot for being insensitive to the terrors of the century. The urban apocalypse of *Little Gidding*, with its evocation of the London bombings, is evidence against that:

After the dark dove with the flickering tongue
   Had passed below the horizon of his homing
   While the dead leaves still rattled on like tin

Over the asphalt where no other sound was
   Between three districts whence the smoke arose
   I met one walking, loitering and hurried
As if blown towards me like the metal leaves
   Before the urban dawn wind unresisting.

                        (II, lines 28–35)[91]

But where Eliot speaks of destruction here in an almost empty voice, there are others who respond to it more passionately.

THE TWENTIETH CENTURY

The distinctively twentieth-century voice of the Anglican spiritual tradition has, I think, left behind the nineteenth century's preoccupation with creating a language to compensate for the triumph of expository prose. This does not mean that that issue had been resolved, only that it was superseded by more urgent matters – the appalling destructiveness of the times. Wilfred Owen is the first of their line. He does not sweeten the slaughter of the First World War with patriotism or high ideals or pious hopes. The first thing that he insists we acknowledge is simply the scale and finality of the killing. The fragmentary 'Preface' that he wrote for a projected volume of war poems asserts that 'This book is not about heroes'. It also insists that 'Above all I am not concerned with Poetry'.[92] Poems such as 'Exposure', 'The Sentry' and 'Smile, Smile, Smile' make an effort to convey the full grimness of the trenches and their aftermath. They offer the reader a kind of perverse incarnation into the worst of human experience – a perversity demanded not by poetic fashion but by the perversity of the world itself.

The churches' willingness to sanctify the war – and indeed their general attachment to the status quo and hatred of the flesh – leaves Owen with only a tenuous attachment to the Christian institution. But he retains a sense of the humanity of Jesus, as in the poem 'At a Calvary Near the Ancre', quoted above, or in 'Soldier's Dream':[93]

> I dreamed kind Jesus fouled the big-gun gears;
> And caused a permanent stoppage in all bolts;
> And buckled with a smile Mausers and Colts;
> And rusted every bayonet with His tears.
>
> And there were no more bombs, of ours or Theirs,
> Not even an old flint-lock, nor even a pikel.
> But God was vexed, and gave all power to Michael;
> And when I woke he'd seen to our repairs.

Jesus, it seems can be trusted. But God cannot. The Christian religion has become so entangled with the patriotic, the sanguinary, the patriarchal that God, like the old man in Owen's 'Parable', would rather continue the killing.

For Owen, hope is very difficult. Perhaps that is the only properly human response in the situation in which he found himself. Like Tennyson, he rejects any easy out that would refer the dead directly to the life of the age to come. First, the reality and irreversibility of death must register itself in our minds and hearts. And the poet must protest the casual acceptance of mass death as an instrument of power. Even if one might maintain some righteousness in the Allied cause (easier perhaps in the Second World War than in the First), Owen saw in the resort to violence itself the critical danger. The thing to be hoped and prayed for was that God would not allow the violence to become part of the soul of the West. Addressing a piece of artillery, he says:

> Be not withdrawn, dark arm, thy spoilure done,
> Safe to the bosom of our prosperity.
> But when thy spell be cast complete and whole,
> May God curse thee, and cut thee from our soul![94]

What Owen confronted face to face in the trenches has become the basic reality of twentieth-century life – a world constantly on the brink of destruction. The even vaster destruction of the Second World War, the introduction and multiplication of atomic weapons, the destabilisation of populations by war, famine, and civil upheaval, our increasing awareness of the limits of the planet – all these have combined to make us aware of the finitude of human life. The response of governments, often enough, has been not to deal constructively with the problems, but to turn their weapons on their own citizens for no reason other than the arrogance of power. Owen's fear has been amply realised.

At the same time, all this misery has become a kind of unmentionable secret, which we resolutely refuse to recognise as central to our historical experience. The cultivation of prosperity and a focus on personal well-being – even, ironically, on a very limited kind of spiritual well-being – have helped us to ignore it all. One task for the modern bearers of the poetic tradition of spirituality has been to serve as prophets, to protest against and undermine the forgetfulness, short-sightedness, and denial that characterise our daily lives. John Betjeman was a persistent voice in the middle of the century attacking the modern fantasy that we are a people new-sprung from the earth with no limits, no embarrassing anchor in the grimy, dusty past, indeed no real rooting in the earth. His poetry is often scathingly ironic, as it unveils the fatuity of middle-class or bureaucratic self-deception. His wrath rises in part out of his own strong sense of the vital human connection with past and with place. His poem 'St Saviour's, Aberdeen Park, Highbury, London, N.'[95] announces the importance of that specificity of place in its long title, and the poem reiterates it with its description (in hexameters!) of the journey there:

> With oh such peculiar branching and over-reaching of wire
>   Trolley-bus standards pick their threads from the
>   London sky
> Diminishing up the perspective . . . (lines 1–3)

The speaker describes the neighbourhood as it was when his parents lived there and as it is at the time of writing, not long after the end of World War II. The centre of it is the parish church and its centre the reserved sacrament. In the language of Anglo-Catholic piety, Betjeman's speaker describes the paradox that unifies it all for him:

> Wonder beyond Time's wonders, that Bread so white and
>   small
> Veiled in golden curtains, too mighty for men to see,
> Is the Power that sends the shadows up this polychrome
>   wall,
> Is God who created the present, the chain-smoking
>   millions and me;
> Beyond the throb of the engines is the throbbing heart of
>   all –
> Christ, at this Highbury altar, I offer myself to Thee.
>
> (lines 31–6)

This is no piety that takes one away from the world. The very point is to be immersed in it – not just in some isolated present, but in a whole succession of moments in the life of the world: the moving shadows, the chain-smoking millions, and all. To be connected to God is to be connected to the universe through its throbbing heart.

W. H. Auden has perhaps been the single most characteristic voice of the Anglican poetic tradition in the twentieth century: learned, colloquial, devout, irreverent, political, apolitical. He has taken on many colourings in different moments and settings; yet, there is a core of clear-eyed willingness to look at life as it is, in all its irreducible unintelligibility, and somehow to see it in the light of grace. The poem 'Whitsunday at Kirchstetten',[96] written in 1962, sums up many of his recurrent themes. It is prefaced by a line from a second-century apocryphon called the *Acts of John*; the speaker is Jesus:

> *Grace dances. I would pipe. Dance ye all.*

From there, the poem narrates the experience and musings of an Anglo-American Anglican worshipping at an Austrian Roman Catholic Eucharist on the feast of Pentecost, which celebrates the giving of the Spirit. The ambiguities of the moment are acknowledged. The friendliness of the local people owes something to the Allied victory less than twenty years before and to the strength of the American dollar. But grace, after all, is always undeserved. That is the whole point of the Eucharist, where the 'Body of the Second Adam' is offered to his enemies and ours. Auden reminds us that the Eastern Bloc, after all, was only a few miles away, so unlike the West and yet so like.

And what does Auden make, in this context, of the miracle of Pentecost, the speaking in tongues? He turns it on its head and makes it a hearing in tongues instead,[97] which can then lead to a repristinisation of our language:

> Rejoice: we who were born
>   congenitally deaf are able
> to listen now to rank outsiders. The Holy Ghost
>   does not abhor a golfer's jargon,
> a Lower-Austrian accent, the cadences even
>   of my own little Anglo-American
> musico-literary set . . .
>   . . .
> . . . but no sacred nonsense can stand Him.
>   Our magical syllables melt away,
> our tribal formulae are laid bare: since this morning,
>   it is with a vocabulary
> made wholesomely profane, open in lexicons
>   to our foes to translate, that we endeavor
> each in his idiom to express the true *magnalia*
>   which need no hallowing from us . . . (lines 32–8, 40–7)

The gift of grace transcends human division in a way that we cannot control or even predict. And it will have much to transcend. In lines that seem prescient of the changing world since then, Auden identifies the challenge of race as critical for the future and acknowledges the guilt of his own kind. Yet he does not offer formulae for the transformation of the planet – rather a counsel to remain alert to God's workings:

> about
> catastrophe or how to behave in one

what do I know, except what everyone knows –
if there when Grace dances, I should dance. (lines 74–7)

The treacheries, the sins, the dangers of the twentieth century
are fully in view here, yet do not force the speaker into despair.
There is always something more, even in catastrophe, to be
expected, to be recognised, to be joined with in the great dance
of Grace. It is not an easy hope; but it is a hope nonetheless.

A comparable steadiness of vision characterises two other
poets whom I have already cited extensively in this study:
R. S. Thomas and Judith Wright. Both have lived lives of
political activism as well as dedication to poetry, Thomas in
the cause of Welsh self-determination and Wright on behalf of
Aboriginal rights and of ecology in her native Australia. Even
without that knowledge, however, one would be able to recognise in their poetic works their realism about the world in which
we live and their determination to remind others of what is at
stake.

R. S. Thomas speaks from the perspective of the exploited and
colonised – indeed, of England's oldest colony, Wales. Yet, he
speaks with the awkward awareness that he is also deeply
English, in language and religious presuppositions, and therefore one of the colonising 'others', as well. His purpose, it seems,
is to see things as they are, which means seeing them in the
lights of both God's absence and God's presence, not denying
the evil and the ugliness, yet remaining open to the advent
of the Holy in the most unexpected of contexts.

Judith Wright has written more than once from the perspective of the mother who must see her children out into a world
increasingly desperate and dangerous. The Atomic Age, where

Bombs ripen on the leafless tree
under which the children play,[98]

is simply the context of our day-to-day existence. Faith and love
are therefore more and not less necessary. The worst foreseeable
future must not entirely erase our awareness that there was

good implicit in our created life, however cut short by human wrongdoing. It is still a time to hope and to write and to work:

> One crack in a grey wall
> can spread
> one seed can grow.
> Don't you understand
> that a minute gained
> might mean
> everything?[99]

In the works of R. S. Thomas or Judith Wright, we are a long way from the gentler poetry of George Herbert. Their poetry is closer to that of Henry Vaughan in that it holds out to us little hope of a political or religious sort. Yet they remain within a tradition of spiritual riches, a tradition that offers hope by affirming the reality of the experience of grace and drawing from it the strength to continue in the journey of human life. The supreme gift of the poet in this tradition is to capture something of this fleeting reality as it enters briefly into our human awareness. Like the brief trail a subatomic particle makes as it passes through a cloud chamber, a poem can provide a trace of the fragile, fleeting, yet profoundly powerful and life-giving experience of divine presence. The poetic analogue helps to sustain us in times of absence, points us a direction to look, trains our eyes to recognise the dance of grace when we see it, nerves us to join in it.

The spirituality thus incarnate in the poem necessarily offers less than a complete set of directions for the reader. It is not a map. But it can serve as a road-sign pointing the general direction; it can offer a rough sketch of a landmark or two. At best, it can even act as a friend standing alongside at the moment of your own discovery of grace and helping you understand where you have come. To some seekers on the spiritual path, this will seem rather a meagre offering; to others, it is all we could have hoped for – and a blessing great enough to be received with thanks and rejoicing. It is the reminder that we can expect to continue being surprised by God's love.

PROSPECT

Part of reflecting about any living tradition must be to look forward at the challenges that it will have to deal with in its continuing development. In some ways, it may be that the world is becoming a friendlier environment for this Anglican tradition of spirituality in and through lyric poetry. The readership for poetry remains small. But the turn into a post-modern world suggests to many people that the monarchy of scientific prose is over. We are more aware than our parents or grandparents that, while we can view the world only from specific perspectives, no single vantage point is so well situated that you can see everything from it at once. We may be friendlier to the idea, at least, that a diversity of voices in conversation can yield more insight than a single voice in monologue. There is room, increasingly, for spirituality – and perhaps room for poetry as well.

And we continue to hear strong voices who play out the deepest possible interactions with God in their poetry. To take a single example, the American poet Louise Glück has the ability to plunge us into a conversation with God before we are quite aware of what is going on, to take us through the pain and astonishment of resurrection without ever giving us the chance to take a detached intellectual stance for or against some doctrine.[1] The compelling authenticity of her voice identifies her (paradoxically, from a modern perspective) as bearer of a tradition that goes back to Donne and Herbert as well as a highly original poet in her own right. The ongoing power of a tradition that could make its way through the dry places of the Enlightenment, the thin air of nineteenth-century scientism, and the killing fields of the modern age, is finding itself incarnate yet again in a new set of human circumstances. The tradition of English-language lyric poetry is alive and well at the turn of the millennia – and so, within that tradition, is the tradition of poetic spirituality.

New circumstances, however, bring new challenges. If the key issue of post-modern life is 'difference', the recognition that modernity has not succeeded in wiping out human divergence, it is far from clear what we will do about that. Will the post-modern world be a peaceful celebration of diversity? Or will it be the bleeding remnants of Yugoslavia replicated endlessly across the world? Or will it be a world in which we turn our backs on one another's particularity and live in gated communities of the like-minded? Will the poetry of spirituality become a common voice to acknowledge and express our difference? Or will it be seen as one more marginal voice among many – the sort of thing that you would like if you like that sort of thing? At least, I do not believe it has in it the resources to become a banner for hostile parties; and for this I am thankful.

The continuing power of the Anglican poetic tradition depends on the fact that it does not seek power. It gives no prescriptions; it does not compel.[2] It springs out of the gospel of Jesus, but remains blessedly free of theology's a priori concern to nail everything down and make sure that others toe the line. It is able to listen to people of other religion and of none and to hear the voice of God there, too. It is able to speak in terms that connect with our human experience, and it invites a sharing of things that lie, as Wordsworth wrote, 'too deep for tears'. It connects with the human world and the world beyond humanity. It invites us, with Vaughan, to rise up, weeping and singing, into the great circle of light where our life-experience at last begins to have full meaning. That also means, of course, that it invites us to see our own poverty and sin and to experience, in the absence of God, how truly empty life can be. But it invites us to this experience of loss precisely so that we can delight fully in the unpredictable but certain experience of God's presence and the fullness of connection and life that it makes possible.

If the poetic voices of spirituality seem alive and well at present, however, the case of Anglicanism as a community or an institution may not be quite so clear. The Anglican Communion now comprises churches far beyond the British Isles, whether in lands settled by British emigrants or in lands formerly colonised by English-speaking powers or in lands to which it has spread through contiguity or through intentional missionising. This expansion involves a variety of social and cultural shifts that make contemporary Anglicanism a complex and sometimes discordant phenomenon. Continuing growth in the Anglican provinces of the Third World and a new level of independence on their part have brought this complexity into the heart of Anglican experience where it cannot be denied or glossed over. Anglicanism speaks in more voices than it did as recently as two or three decades ago. It is unlikely that a consensus about Anglicanism will emerge in the near future; it will be a high achievement if we can simply live together through the time of discernment that lies ahead of us.

The role of our poetic spirituality in this mix is important, but also unpredictable. I suspect that the strongest force in dissuading Anglicans over the centuries from seeking a strong theology and polity like that of other Christian traditions has been the poetic awareness of how much we can never truly know or express. Yet the poetic tradition has barely merited mention in most surveys of what Anglicanism is and means. As A. M. Allchin has put it, 'Anglicans are heirs to a tradition of which at the present they are often almost unaware.'[3] Anglicans are as ready as other Christians to commit idolatry by absolutising our favourite doctrines and rituals – but in our case, this has taken the form of a kind of internal sectarianism rather than overt schism. Anglo-Catholics, Evangelicals, Liberal Catholics, Broad Church folk, Prayer Book strict-constructionists – each party's absolutising of its distinctive peculiarities, of course, also has the reductionist effect of denying the actual diversity within Anglicanism. In the bosom of one's own party, it is possible to be an Anglican without being aware of how fuzzy the boundaries of Anglicanism really are. The discovery of Anglican diversity can be a considerable shock for some.

The great danger of such absolutism and reductionism, of course, is idolatry or, to use the more common contemporary term, fundamentalism. Fundamentalism confuses the means with the end, mistakes the tools with which God reaches out to humanity for the God who reaches out. Fundamentalism may proclaim a Bible that is more absolute than truth, wiser than Jesus, more certain than God's own self – for God, after all, is reported to change his mind on occasion. It may equally well proclaim an inerrant Book of Common Prayer (whether of 1662 or 1928) or an infallible doctrine of ordination or God's eternal disfavour toward people unlike oneself. All these forms of fundamentalism find homes within Anglicanism. They sometimes join forces if, for the moment, they can identify a common enemy.[4] But if our internal sectarians ever succeed in gaining control of Anglicanism, they will end by destroying it. The logic of their exclusive claims will force them to it.

If Anglicanism survives, it will be by the grace of God communicated through the spirituality of the poets. The poets summon us to turn our attention not to the details of church life but to the reality of God's presence, to the surprise of grace. In so doing, they are telling us to abandon idolatry, to abandon fundamentalism, to allow no sacred thing, however venerable, to stand on a level with God's own self, given to us in grace. The poetry we have been exploring here is not the only vehicle by which this spirituality is communicated among us. Quite the contrary, it is a tradition deeply embedded in Anglicanism and spread, like most spirituality, contagiously from one person to another, among those who do not read poetry as much as among those who do. Still, the embodiment of this tradition in lyric poetry gives it additional scope and historical depth and adds the authority of multiple witnesses. The fact that it exists in the written analogues of poetry means that it can continue to communicate with great intensity even when, for whatever reason, it is not thriving in the Anglican church of a given time and place.

If Anglicanism is to survive as a communion – that is, in maintaining actual communion among its very diverse members across the world – it will do so only by acknowledging the centrality of its spiritual tradition. In so far as it can do so, the poetic tradition of spirituality will continue to lodge with it, to contribute to the life of the community, and perhaps also to draw strength from it. In so far as we decline to do so, we shall probably try to substitute, at the heart of Anglicanism, the kind of doctrinal and disciplinary rigidity that we have both rejected and coveted in the Reformed and Roman traditions. If we do so, we will tear Anglicanism, both as community and as tradition, into increasingly smaller pieces.[5]

The poetic tradition of Anglican spirituality arose in the aftermath of the English Reformation. To a great extent, the early poets set its direction and the issues around which it still centres; and they were firmly embedded in the ecclesial context of the Church of England. Still, it is appropriate to raise one further question. It is a very 'Anglican' question to have to ask, for it deals precisely with the evanescence of Anglicanism, the tendency of Anglicanism to disappear if one demands that it sit for its portrait – a tendency as maddening to Anglicans as to anyone else. Since the tradition of Anglican spiritual poetry overlaps so broadly with the canon of English lyric poetry, one must eventually ask, What does all this really have to do with Anglicanism?

Even for those poets who were self-identified as Anglicans one may ask how significant their denominational heritage was for their poetry. George Herbert's poetry was as popular among Dissenters as among members of the Church of England.[6] Perhaps a given poet's place in the literary tradition of the English lyric is as informative as where the person went to church – or whether they did at all. By the same token, one might ask whether some non-Anglican poets are really so different from the Anglicans. Emily Dickinson is at home in this tradition, though I have reluctantly excluded her from this study to avoid muddying categories. Gerard Manley Hopkins left the Church of England for Rome; yet much of his poetry – the

part that is not marked by peculiarly Roman Catholic themes –
fits easily within the Anglican tradition. Is that because of his
Anglican upbringing or because, by the late nineteenth century,
this was simply how one wrote the poetry of spirituality in
English, no matter what one's religious denomination? The
late-twentieth-century novelist and poet, Paul Monette, did not
describe himself as a believer; but, in some sense, it was particularly the Episcopal Church to which he did not go. Where does
that put him in relation to this tradition? His *Love Alone* stands
in the tradition of Vaughan and Tennyson, giving frank voice to
the pain of loss and absence.[7] And in much of the English-
speaking world, denominational affiliation has become officially
irrelevant to such public matters as poetry. The poet Louise
Glück, whom I mentioned above, puts no denominational label
on herself or her poetry. I have no idea what that label would be
if she did. It does not seem profoundly important.

It would be inappropriate and perhaps a bit un-Anglican to
lay claim to all such writers as if they were 'Anglicans unawares'
– inappropriate because insufficiently attentive to their individual experience, un-Anglican because it would suggest a level
of definition for Anglicanism that does not in fact exist. The
point, then, is not to identify a 'pure' Anglican canon, but rather
to recognise that the very refusal of definition that is characteristic of Anglicanism has in fact facilitated the merging of the
Anglican poetic stream into the larger tide of English literature.
As Anglicanism was the unmarked form of post-Reformation
English Christianity, the form that could be taken for granted,
it pervades the literature of the English language, not only that
written in England itself but all the literatures descended from
it. One can accept this fact, however, and still suggest that it is
important to notice where the roots are planted and ask whether
the plant might still gather nourishment from some of its old
rootrun.

The poetic tradition of spirituality that we have been discussing here is no longer dependent in any obvious way on
Anglicanism. Indeed, Anglican churches may need the tradition
more than the tradition needs the churches. This tradition is a

carrier of our soul, without which even the most splendid of bodies – stone-ribbed, glass-walled, gilt, well-musicked, thronged with worshippers – will be dead. This does not mean that Anglicanism can assert some rights over the poetic tradition or that it is free to reclaim it by fiat. There is no ownership of grace. Even God possesses it only in order to give it away. At most Anglicanism can offer itself as a hospitable way station. To do so means to become humbly aware that God works in and with us not because of our own excellence but because of God's generosity.

The uniqueness of Anglicanism is that it has no uniqueness. Let it offer itself then as ongoing home to a spirituality that knows nothing except grace, holds nothing certain except that we will be surprised by life. We cannot really say much more than W. H. Auden does:

> about
> catastrophe or how to behave in one
> what do I know, except what everyone knows –
> if there when Grace dances, I should dance.[8]

As we learn to do that, we shall find, with George Herbert, that however early we arise to celebrate Easter Day, Jesus is there ahead of us, bringing even better provisions to the festivities than we.

NOTES

Introduction

1. The tendency to insularity and even intellectual xenophobia is a fundamental temptation of academic communities. In acknowledging this, I do not mean to dismiss the importance of literary scholarship as such. In fact, literary scholars preserved and studied this heritage when theological scholars and ecclesiastics were showing little interest in it, as A. M. Allchin observed in his essay 'Anglican spirituality', p. 318.

2. I am trying to capture some of the difference of approach that A. M. Allchin speaks of in connection with ways of studying scripture. He acknowledges the value of the 'scientific study of the original texts', but also says, 'To hear the scriptures read in a community of prayer and praise is to receive another and no less valid impression of the meaning than that which we receive through their academic study. It is to learn to hear the words with our bodies as well as our minds.' *The World is a Wedding: Explorations in Christian Spirituality*, p. 18.

3. Wright is a useful example of the ill-defined boundaries of this tradition. Her poems contain references to Christian belief and ritual of a sort that may most easily be taken as evidence of Anglican influence in her early years. As an adult, she seems to have avoided formal religion and framed her beliefs more readily in Jungian terms. See Veronica Brady, *South of My Days: A Biography of Judith Wright*, pp. 425–6. Yet her poetry fits very well with the mainstream of the tradition examined here.

1. A Poetic Spirituality

1. By 'priesthood' I mean the complex of human and divine interactions I wrote of in *Living on the Border of the Holy: Renewing the Priesthood of All* (Harrisburg, PA: Morehouse Publishing, 1999), pp. 3–32.

2. I could content myself with one such term, 'God', since that is the most characteristic usage of Christianity. But even that term can be misleading. One can use it (or hear it) in a quasi-Gnostic sense as if it referred to a Being who is divorced from or even opposed to the rest of reality that we know, the earthly material reality in which we partici-

pate. (The fact that such interpretations were ruled out in the early Christian creeds has not kept them from being available or even, at times, dominant in subsequent Christian history.) Or again 'God' may be used as if it referred to a Being who is externally related to the rest of reality – rather like the Greek gods except that there is only One in the Christian pantheon – rather than a Being who radically shapes all reality, who is, indeed, Way, Truth, Life, the I AM at the heart of everything.

3. 'Between one unknown and the other, there is here no representational knowledge, no "metaphysics", but only a mode of ascent which receives something of the infinite source so long as it goes on receiving it . . .'. John Milbank, *The Word Made Strange: Theology, Language, Culture*, pp. 44–5.

4. Catullus 5; the translation is mine.

5. The tradition goes back at least to Origen in the third century, and it was a major element in the Western Middle Ages when the Song of Songs was a focus of Christian reading and comment and manuscripts of it outnumbered those of other biblical books. See Wilfred Cantwell Smith, *What Is Scripture? A Comparative Approach* (Minneapolis: Fortress Press, 1993), pp. 22–34. The tradition was still alive and well in the eighteenth century as shown by Edward Moore's libretto for William Boyce's 'serenata' (oratorio) *Solomon*, which can be read either erotically or spiritually with equal ease.

6. Robert Herrick, *The Poetical Works*, ed. F. W. Moorman (London: Oxford University Press, 1921), p. 256.

7. Martin Thornton, *English Spirituality: An Outline of Ascetical Theology According to the English Pastoral Tradition*, pp. 230–56. Interestingly, Thornton does not deal with poetry as such.

8. Indeed, T. S. Eliot found it easy to incorporate a few lines from one of Lancelot Andrewes' Christmas sermons into the opening of his 'Journey of the Magi'. Ellen Davis notes the shift away from this mode of preaching at the close of the seventeenth century in *Imagination Shaped: Old Testament Preaching in the Anglican Tradition*, pp. 2–3.

9. Smith, *What is Scripture?* pp. 34–5.

10. In a larger sense, one can say that '*Poesis* . . . is an integral aspect of Christian practice and redemption. Its work is the ceaseless re-narrating and "explaining" of human history under the sign of the cross'. Milbank, *The Word Made Strange*, p. 32.

11. M. R. Ritley.

12. One Bishop Pearson (seventeenth-century?) is quoted as saying that they were not intended to be 'a complete body of divinity' and contrasting them with both the Canons of Trent and continental confessions that were 'controversial, diffuse, and longsome'. See E. J. Bicknell, *A Theological Introduction to the Thirty-Nine Articles of the Church of England*, 3rd edn revised H. J. Carpenter (London: Longmans, 1955), p. 17.

13. See, most notably, *Tract 90* of *Tracts for the Times*: *Remarks on Certain Passages in the Thirty-nine Articles* by John Henry Newman, originally published in 1841.

14. Paul Avis notes that Whitgift and Hooker dedicated themselves to resisting the puritan view that 'a form of church government was contained in the gospel' (*Anglicanism and the Christian Church: Theological Resources in Historical Perspective*, p. 307).

15. 'Anglicans do not live by a system but rather live in a tradition' (Robert Runcie, 'Christian thinking: the Anglican tradition of thoughtful holiness'). Harvey H. Guthrie has suggested a threefold typology of churches: confessional, experiential and pragmatic, and places Anglicanism in the third type because 'the questions with which Anglicans are characteristically concerned are pragmatic questions'. See his essay 'Anglican spirituality: an ethos and some issues', p. 3.

16. This could also mean, in practice, that it was the lazy choice and the choice that the religious enthusiast would tend to find wanting. Thomas Hardy captures something of the situation in the figure of Coggan, who admits that chapel folk are more religious, but says, 'I hate a feller who'll change his old ancient doctrines for the sake of getting to heaven. I'd as soon turn king's-evidence for the few pounds you get' (*Far from the Madding Crowd*, ch. 42).

17. On the Roman Catholic side, one sometimes finds poetry dedicated largely to the emphasising of boundary issues distinguishing Roman from Anglican Christianity, for example the later poems of Richard Crashaw or John Henry Newman's *Dream of Gerontius*. The more radical forms of protestantism, on the other hand, seem to have been most at home in expository prose. For the shift to an unadorned prose rhetoric, see Perry Miller, 'The plain style', pp. 147–86.

18. Patrick Mauney, quoted by Ian Douglas, who continues, 'We need not apologize for our Anglican identity lying in "who gets invited to what meetings." For at the heart of such identity is a profound affirmation of relationship originating in the incarnation and lived out when "two or three are gathered together in my name" ' ('The changing face of world Anglicanism', *The Witness* 81/5 (May 1998), pp. 10–11).

2. Resources of Image and Language

1. Morning and Evening Prayer were long the predominant experience of public worship for most Anglicans, though they are currently superseded in many places by the Eucharist.

2. Cf. W. C. Smith's observation of the importance of worship as the context for scripture in Anglicanism: 'Among Christians, Anglicans . . . approximate more closely than . . . other Protestants to those many religious movements around the world in which patterns of the service are spiritually more important than patterns of ideas. In

their case, a written form for that pattern can seem as important as written scripture' (*What is Scripture?*, p. 205).

3. Matthew Arnold gave theoretical expression to this quality of biblical language in the nineteenth century. 'The language of the Bible is not to be confused with the language of science. Biblical language is not "rigid and fixed" but "fluid, passing, literary"; it is language "thrown out," as Arnold was so often to remark' (James C. Livingston, *Matthew Arnold and Christianity: His Religious Prose Writings*, p. 43).

4. 1 Corinthians 13:7–8; Ezekiel 11:19.

5. George Herbert, *The Country Parson, The Temple*, ed. John N. Wall, Jr, (New York: Paulist Press, 1981), pp. 305–6.

6. Exodus 15:2–3.

7. 1 John 4:8, 16.

8. Judith Wright, *Collected Poems: 1942–85* (Sydney: Angus & Robertson, 1994), p. 52.

9. Henry Vaughan, *The Complete Poems*, ed. Alan Rudrum (New Haven: Yale University Press, 1981), pp. 310–11.

10. 'Holy Scripture containeth all things necessary to salvation: so that whatsoever is not read therein, nor may be proved thereby, is not to be required of any man, that it should be believed as an article of the Faith, or be thought requisite or necessary to salvation' (Articles of Religion VI).

11. 'This relationship between literature and faith implicit in the liturgy becomes explicit in the tradition of Anglican poetry and prose; in the series of distinctly theological poets, from John Donne . . . to . . . R. S. Thomas in our own day.' A. M. Allchin, 'Anglican spirituality', p. 315.

12. Herbert, p. 305.

13. Vaughan, p. 311.

14. Vaughan, p. 296–8.

15. Thomas Traherne, *Selected Poems and Prose*, ed. Alan Bradford (London: Penguin, 1991), p. 103.

16. 'Covenanters: Paul', lines 1–4, in R. S. Thomas, *Collected Poems: 1945–1990* (London: Phoenix Giant, 1995), p. 406. In Acts 9:5, Jesus replies to Paul, 'I am Jesus whom thou persecutest: it is hard for thee to kick against the pricks.'

17. Coleridge recognised that the biblical authors 'worked through the imagination' (R. L. Brett, *Faith and Doubt: Religion and Secularization in Literature from Wordsworth to Larkin*, p. 52. This did not contradict his understanding of the Bible's authority and seems well in tune with earlier practice if not necessarily earlier theory.

18. W. H. Auden, *Collected Poems*. ed. Edward Mendelson (New York: Random House, 1976 and London: Faber & Faber, 1976 and 1991), p. 289.

19. L. Wm. Countryman, *Living on the Border of the Holy*, pp. 33–46.

20. Herbert, p. 168. It may be objected that Herbert also wrote:

> Though private prayer be a brave design,
> Yet public hath more promises, more love.
> *(The Church Porch*, lines 397–8)

These lines, however, are preparatory to the spiritual journey outlined in the main body of Herbert's collection of poems, which leads through the ceremonies of the church, without ever disparaging them, to a more intimate relationship with God.

21. Vaughan, pp. 181–2.
22. John Betjeman, *Collected Poems*, enlarged edn (Boston: Houghton Mifflin, 1971), pp. 138–43.
23. Auden, pp. 558–9.
24. Christina Rossetti, *Poems and Prose*, ed. Jan Marsh (London: J. M. Dent, Everyman, 1994), p. 174.
25. Herbert, p. 156.
26. Vaughan, p. 306–7.
27. Joseph H. Summers holds that Vaughan's passion for the natural world, if not his use of it, would have marked him as novel in his own day (*The Heirs of Donne and Jonson*, p. 122).
28. Vaughan, pp. 188–9.
29. Vaughan's quotation is in Latin and includes the phrase *exerto capito* (sic), 'with raised head', echoed in line 3.
30. Christopher Smart, *The Collected Poems*, ed. Norman Callan (London: Routledge & Kegan Paul, 1949), vol. 1, pp. 352, 367.
31. Smart, p. 311.
32. William Wordsworth, *The Complete Poetical Works* (Boston: Houghton Mifflin, 1904), p. 285.
33. *Samuel Taylor Coleridge*, ed. H. J. Jackson (New York: Oxford University Press, 1985), p. 55.
34. Coleridge, p. 50.
35. Coleridge, p. 55.
36. *Later Life: A Double Sonnet of Sonnets* 21, Rossetti, p. 245.
37. Wright, pp. 127–9.
38. Thomas, p. 426.
39. 'Holy Baptism (II)', lines 6–7, 15, Herbert, p. 158.
40. Vaughan, pp. 172–3.
41. Vaughan, pp. 288–9.
42. Thomas Traherne, *Centuries* (New York: Harper & Brothers, 1960), 3.2–4, pp. 109–12.
43. There is no possibility that Wordsworth knew Traherne's *Centuries*. which lay unpublished and unrecognised until this century. His perspective may, however, owe something to the Platonism that was common in English education and which Vaughan also made use of (cf. his phrase 'my second race' in 'The Retreat', referring to the Platonic idea of pre-existence of the soul).
44. 'Intimations of Immortality from Recollections of Early Childhood', lines 59–67, Wordsworth, p. 354.

45. 'Intimations of Immortality', lines 149–57, 162–8, Wordsworth, p. 355.
46. 'Reading Thomas Traherne,' Wright, pp. 206–7.
47. Wright, pp. 238–9. Jennifer Strauss sees the eucharistic reference in this poem as 'too perfunctory to carry poetic conviction'. See *Judith Wright*, p. 80. But the power of the image will vary depending on the depth and complexity of associations that it evokes in the reader.

3. Presence and Absence

1. George Herbert, *The Country Parson, The Temple*, ed. John N. Wall, Jr (New York: Paulist Press, 1981), pp. 278–9.
2. Herbert, pp. 166–7.
3. James 2:23.
4. Thomas Gray, in his *Elegy Written in a Country Church-Yard* uses this same language of friendship to describe a life that was fully human, fully rewarding and rewarded, though lived in a kind of obscurity that contrasted sharply with the value the eighteenth century placed on public life and education.
5. See pp. 49–50.
6. 'Mysticism' is notoriously difficult to define. C. P. M. Jones has offered a useful definition that speaks of 'four constants in mystical experience', which include – in very abbreviated form – (1) contact beyond the sensual with an 'object', (2) the inexhaustibility of this 'object', (3) the immediacy of the contact, and (4) the inward affinity between the 'object' and the person. See his 'Mysticism, human and divine', pp. 19–20.
7. See p. 55.
8. Henry Vaughan, *The Complete Poems*, ed. Alan Rudrum (New Haven, CT: Yale University Press, 1976), p. 370.
9. Stevie Davies, *Henry Vaughan*, p. 12.
10. Vaughan, p. 179.
11. Davies, *Henry Vaughan*, p. 135.
12. Thomas Traherne, *Selected Poems and Prose*, ed. Alan Bradford (London: Penguin, 1991), pp. 58–60.
13. The metaphor of inebriation goes back at least to Alexandrian Judaism. In the Old Greek version of the Psalms, the equivalent of Psalm 23:5 ('my cup runneth over', AV) is rendered 'your cup renders one utterly intoxicated'. The theme of sober drunkenness is found henceforward in the literature of mysticism.
14. Judith Wright, *Collected Poems 1942–1985* (Sydney: Angus & Robertson, 1994), pp. 331–2.
15. Alfred Tennyson, *In Memoriam* (Chicago: Henneberry, n.d.), pp. 56–7.
16. Tennyson, *In Memoriam*, pp. 109–10.
17. Herbert, p. 316.
18. John Donne, *The Complete Poetry and Selected Prose*, ed. Charles M. Coffin (New York: The Modern Library, 1952), pp. 271–2.

19. Christina Rossetti, *Poems*, selected by Peter Washington (New York: Alfred A. Knopf, 1993), p. 221.
20. Christina Rossetti, *Poems and Prose*, ed. Jan Marsh (London: J. M. Dent, Everyman, 1994), p. 109.
21. Rossetti, *Poems and Prose*, p. 128.
22. Stevie Smith, *A Selection*, ed. Hermione Lee (London: Faber & Faber, 1983), pp. 147–8.
23. T. S. Eliot, *Collected Poems 1909–1962* (New York: Harcourt Brace & Co., 1963 and London: Faber & Faber, 1963), p. 207.
24. Herbert, p. 284.
25. Augustine, *Confessions* 1.1.
26. Tennyson later identified the poet as Goethe: see *Tennyson, A Selected Edition*, ed. Christopher Ricks (Berkeley: University of California Press, 1989). p. 344n.
27. Tennyson, *In Memoriam*, pp. 6–7.
28. Herbert, pp. 160–2.
29. Elizabeth Barrett Browning, *The Poetical Works* (Chicago: Belford, Clarke & Co., n.d.), pp. 605–7.
30. Rossetti, *Poems and Prose*, p. 111.
31. Donne, p. 248.
32. Gerard Manley Hopkins, *The Poems*, 4th edn, ed. W. H. Gardner and N. H. MacKenzie (London: Oxford University Press, 1979), p. 101.
33. Herbert, pp. 197–8.
34. Vaughan, pp. 224–5.
35. Rossetti, *Poems and Prose*, pp. 113–14.
36. R. S. Thomas, *Collected Poems 1945–1990* (London: Macmillan), p. 180.
37. Thomas, p. 361.
38. Thomas, p. 517.
39. W. H. Auden, *Collected Poems*, ed. Edward Mendelson (New York: Random House, 1976 and London: Faber & Faber, 1976 and 1991), pp. 558–9.

4. Living by Grace

1. George Herbert, *The Country Parson, The Temple*, ed. John N. Wall, Jr (New York: Paulist Press, 1981), pp. 311–12.
2. Above, p. 69.
3. Article XI: ' . . . that we are justified by Faith only, is a most wholesome Doctrine, and very full of comfort . . .'
4. Good works are, to be sure, a good thing as opposed to a bad thing (a phrase I owe to Joseph L. McInerney). But that is not the issue here. The issue is what kind of reliance human beings place in themselves. We are always tempted to claim to be in charge of our own salvation in ways that are absurdly improbable.
5. Robert Herrick, *The Poetical Works*, ed. F. W. Moorman (London: Oxford University Press, 1921), p. 329.

6. Douglas Brooks-Davies, in his introduction to the Everyman's Poetry edition of *Robert Herrick* (London: J. M. Dent, 1996), pp. xx–xxi.
7. In fact, 'in the beginning there is God's grace arousing contribution': John E. Booty, 'Contrition in Anglican spirituality: Hooker, Donne and Herbert', p. 27.
8. John Donne, *The Complete Poetry and Selected Prose*, ed. Charles M. Coffin (New York: The Modern Library, 1952), pp. 270–1.
9. Henry Vaughan, *The Complete Poems*, ed. Alan Rudrum (New Haven, CT: Yale University Press, 1976), pp. 206–8.
10. The gourd is that of Jonah 4:6–11, which first offered hope of relief from the sun, but quickly withered.
11. *Samuel Taylor Coleridge*, ed. H. J. Jackson (Oxford: Oxford University Press, 1985), pp. 46–65.
12. W. H. Auden, *Collected Poems*, ed. Edward Mendelson (New York: Random House, 1976 and London: Faber & Faber, 1976 and 1991), p. 466.
13. *Confessions* 8.7.
14. Auden, pp. 129–31.
15. Auden, pp. 454–5.
16. Wilfred Owen, *The Poems*, ed. Jon Stallworthy (New York: W. W. Norton, 1986 and New Directions Publishing Corporation, 1963), p. 158.
17. Jon Stallworthy, editorial note on 'The Kind Ghosts', Owen, p. 158n.
18. Vaughan, pp. 227–8.
19. John Donne, *Devotions upon Emergent Occasions*, ed. Anthony Raspa (New York: Oxford University Press, 1987), pp. 86–7.
20. Herrick, p. 382.
21. Christian Rossetti, *Poems and Prose*, ed. Jan Marsh (London: J. M. Dent, Everyman, 1994), pp. 114–15; Jan Marsh calls our attention to the fact that the title refers to Jeremiah 8:20, p. 439.
22. Rossetti, *Poems and Prose*, p. 122.
23. Judith Wright, *Collected Poems 1942–1985* (Sydney: Angus & Robertson, 1994), pp. 152–3.
24. Wright, p. 229.
25. Elizabeth Barrett Browning, *The Poetical Works* (Chicago: Belford, Clarke & Co., n.d.), pp. 607–9; stanzas 5–7 are quoted.
26. R. S. Thomas, *Collected Poems 1945–1990* (London: Macmillan), p. 521.
27. Herbert, pp. 311–12.
28. Alfred Tennyson, *In Memoriam* (Chicago: The Henneberry Company, n.d.), xxxvi, p. 34.
29. Matthew Arnold, *Poetical Works*, ed. C. B. Tinker and H. F. Lowry (London: Oxford University Press, 1950), pp. 245–7.
30. So George Herbert in 'Love (I)' and 'Love (II)' (pp. 168–9).
31. Herrick, p. 383.
32. Herrick, p. 279.

33. In his introduction to the Everyman's Poetry edition of *Robert Herrick*, p. xxi.
34. Donne, *Complete Poetry and Selected Prose*, p. 252.
35. Sonnet 14, Donne, *Complete Poetry and Selected Prose*, p. 252.
36. Auden, p. 259.
37. Although Christina's brother William separated her poems, after her death, 'into "religious" and "general" this is a well-nigh impossible task, since most of the "general" poems are as saturated with religion as her religious poems are saturated with thoughts of human love': Frances Thomas, *Christina Rossetti*, pp. 281–2.
38. Rossetti, *Poems and Prose*, p. 126; the poem is untitled. The line 'vanity of vanities' alludes to Ecclesiastes 1:2.
39. Rossetti, *Poems and Prose*, pp. 126–7. The title refers to Paul's preference for celibacy, expressed in 1 Corinthians 7:38. The poem may refer to the death of the poet's sister Maria, who had become a nun, Marsh (ed.), p. 440. But she used a similar motif between lovers in 'The Convent Threshold', and her brother, Dante Gabriel Rossetti's 'The Blessed Damozel' represents a kind of failed version of it.
40. Owen, p. 86. The ceremony he describes should in fact have been performed on Good Friday, not Maundy Thursday. Either Owen misplaced it through unfamiliarity with Roman Catholic liturgy or he was suggesting that kissing the 'warm live hand' was equivalent to receiving the body of Christ, for Maundy Thursday celebrates the institution of the Eucharist.
41. Owen, p. 111. Identifying the priests as those who are 'flesh-marked by the Beast' (cf. Revelation 13:16–18), and as the scribes, identifies them with the enemies of Jesus. The soldiers, on the other hand, may kill, but, according to Owen, they do not hate:

> . . . when every fighter brags
> He fights on Death, for lives; not men, for flags.
> ('The Next War', p. 142, ll. 13–14)

42. Vaughan, pp. 177–8.
43. Vaughan, pp. 208–9.
44. E.g., Galatians 3:27–8.
45. From *Songs of Innocence,* in William Blake, *Blake's Poems and Prophecies*, ed. Max Plowman (London: J. M. Dent, Everyman, 1927), p. 14.
46. Blake, p. 37.
47. The importance of the human community for our poets does not mean that they treated it with an unreflective optimism. George Herbert, for example, in 'The Family' and 'Church Rents and Schisms', treats the human capacity to interfere with and even nullify God's efforts to create a new human community.
48. Barrett Browning, p. 338.
49. Owen, p. 52.

50. William Wordsworth, *The Complete Poetical Works*, ed. Andrew J. George (Boston: Houghton Mifflin, 1904), p. 81.
51. Wright, p. 175.
52. Thomas, p. 525. The poem draws on Revelation for some details of its vision, but counters that work in others, for example 'the unmetalled highways' contrast sharply with John's streets paved with gold. This apocalyptic vision could reside imaginatively in a renewed rural Wales.
53. Thomas, 'Suddenly', lines 1–2, p. 426.
54. The final long poem 'The Church Militant', with its polemics against other forms of Christianity, in some sense stands outside the work proper.
55. Owen, p. 151.
56. He did lay the blame at God's door indirectly in 'Soldier's Dream': 'I dreamed kind Jesus fouled the big-gun gears . . . / But God was vexed, and gave all power to Michael; / And when I woke he'd seen to our repairs.'
57. Thomas, p. 427.
58. T. S. Eliot, *Collected Poems 1909–1962* (New York: Harcourt Brace & Co., 1964 and London: Faber & Faber, 1963), p. 208.
59. Perhaps we can relate this aspect of Anglican spirituality to an element of British culture noted by John Milbank. Having acknowledged that British culture is usually described as 'empiricist, philistine and basely pragmatic', he goes on to argue that 'there is an alternative vatic, "Platonic" tradition within British culture which construes empiricism as openness to the strange and unclassifiable, and pragmatism as surrender to the surprise of that which is mediated through us in language, from a transcendent source': *The Word Made Strange* p. 2.
60. Herbert, p. 139.
61. In this regard, Herbert was not unlike Evelyn Underhill, who insisted that mysticism was 'the basal human experience . . . finding its least inadequate expression in the history and doctrines of Christianity': Susan J. Smalley, 'Evelyn Underhill and the mystical tradition', p. 269.
62. Thomas Traherne, *Selected Poems and Prose*, ed. Alan Bradford (London: Penguin, 1991), p. 110.
63. Vaughan, pp. 155–6.
64. Blake, pp. 346–9.
65. Blake, p. 30.
66. E.g., 'How Do You See?', Smith, pp. 169–74.
67. Stevie Smith, 'The Airy Christ: After reading Dr Rieu's translation of St Mark's Gospel' in *A Selection*, ed. Hermione Lee (London: Faber & Faber, 1983), pp. 141–2.
68. Tennyson, *In Memoriam,* pp. 31–2.
69. 'To the Rev. F. D. Maurice' in Alfred Tennyson, *The Poetic and Dramatic Works* (Boston: Houghton Mifflin Co., 1898), p. 222.

5. A Living Tradition

1. The two were roughly contemporary, though Donne was the elder by twenty years. They had a kind of familial link, as well, Herbert's mother, Lady Magdalen Herbert, having been one of Donne's faithful supporters during his difficult years of relative poverty and exclusion from public preferment. This continued into a mature friendship between the two men. (Izaak Walton, 'The Life of Mr George Herbert' in *The Works of George Herbert in Prose and Verse* (New York: Thomas Y. Crowell & Co., n.d.), pp. 24–7, 35–6.) The first printed editions of most of their poetry appeared in the same year, 1633, in each case after the author's death. Each made a fundamental contribution to the tradition.

2. Paul Avis speaks of a 'state of ideological prelapsarian innocence', in which 'the church just gets on with being the church – believing, worshipping, celebrating, serving – without bothering its head about its identity' (*Anglicanism and the Christian Church*, p. 16). Perhaps this innocence, at least in the form of a dream or a hope, has animated Anglicanism ever since; Avis notes that Archbishop Ussher, a little later, embraced it so far as to propose a joint educational venture in Ireland with the Roman Catholic clergy there (p. 86).

3. The beloved is described as 'the daughter of the Queen of love' (Sonnet 39), with 'an hundred Graces' sitting on each eyelid (40). The poet admonishes her not to fly from him as Daphne from Phoebus (28). He compares his own art unfavourably with that of Arion or Orpheus (38, 44). He treats Eros as a planetary divinity controlling human fate much like Mars (60). There are also moments when he brings the beloved into connection with the Christian understanding of God, treating due worship of her as offered to the God whose image (alluding to Genesis 1:26–7) she bears (61).

4. Edmund Spenser, *Spenser's Minor Poems*, edited Ernest de Sélincourt (Oxford: The Clarendon Press, 1910), p. 405.

5. John Donne, *Complete Poetry and Selected Prose*, ed. Charles M. Coffin (New York: The Modern Library, 1952), p. 209.

6. Donne, *Complete Poetry and Selected Prose*, p. 247.

7. 'It would not be incorrect to refer to the theology of John Donne as the theology of divine mercy . . . Thus, in spite of the persistent penitential tone of his *Devotions* and his Holy Sonnets the focus is not on sin but on love, God's forgiving love arousing the response of love' (John E. Booty, 'Contrition in Anglican spirituality', p. 35).

8. *The Temple* proper begins, after the preliminaries of 'The Church Porch' and 'Superliminare' (a threshold admonition), with 'The Altar', which allegorises the central article of church furnishing, and 'The Sacrifice', a longish poem placed on the lips of Jesus and narrating the Passion. The combination of the two alludes to the sacrament of

the Holy Communion; and the eucharistic feast thus prefigures the more intimate banquet of the soul as Love's guest in 'Love (III)'.

9. 'Instead of being "about religion," [Herbert's] poems are the reflections and creations of a religious life: the hymns, complaints, cries, laments, examinations, quarrels, rejoicing, and promises of a talented poet who was most concerned with the relation of his experience to God's works and Word' (Joseph H. Summers, *The Heirs of Donne and Johnson*, p. 97).

10. This is not to dismiss the importance of the 'preliminaries'. 'I think we may read [the poems] better if, by means of an attentive reading of "The Church-porch," we have come to realize how firmly Herbert's worship and self-examination were grounded in the ordinary events of daily life and a concern for the selves of others. He is the least solipsistic of poets' (Summers, *The Heirs of Donne and Johnson*, p. 99).

11. Barbara Kiefer Lewalski argues that 'Calvinism provided a detailed chart of the spiritual life for Elizabethan and 17th-century English Protestants', including the major religious poets (*Protestant Poetics and the Seventeenth-Century Religious Lyric*, p. 14). She also acknowledges, however, that English Calvinists were often more 'inclined to moderation and ambiguity' than their Continental counterparts (p. 20).

12. Barbara Kiefer Lewalski reads 'The Water Course' as an endorsement of double predestination (*Protestant Poetics and the Seventeenth-Century Religious Lyric*, p. 25). It is a possible reading, but not inevitable; the poem remains ambiguous.

13. George Herbert, *The Country Parson, The Temple*, ed. John N. Wall (New York: Paulist Press, 1981), pp. 165–6.

14. Interestingly, this poem provided a kind of 'table of contents' for Christopher Bryant's *The Heart in Pilgrimage: Christian Guidelines for the Human Journey*, a Jungian interpretation of Christian spirituality by an Anglican author.

15. The centrality of such a vision to all Christian spirituality explains Elizabeth Clarke's observation that Herbert has appealed to readers of all religious parties, all of whom have tried to claim him for their own: 'George Herbert's *The Temple*: The genius of Anglicanism and the inspiration for poetry', pp. 128–30.

16. Herrick lived long enough to see the restoration of the monarchy and himself to his previous position.

17. 'Mainstream' Anglicans and Puritans were not so far apart as we have sometimes assumed; their theologies overlapped in many ways; see Gordon S. Wakefield, 'The Puritans', pp. 437–45. Still they certainly drew sharp distinctions between the two groups at the time, and their legacies have led in different directions; see Paul Avis, *Anglicanism and the Christian Church*, pp. 79–89.

18. Robert Herrick, *The Poetical Works*, ed. F. W. Moorman (London: Oxford University Press, 1921), p. 5.

19. He assumes the same stance in the second poem, 'To His Muse', where he advises her (ironically, given that all this is going to press) to stay at home, since her rural and pastoral concerns will not meet with the favour of the educated and important (Herrick, pp. 5–6).

20. 'A Thanksgiving to God for His House', lines 37–40 (Herrick, pp. 339–41).

21. Henry Vaughan, *The Complete Poems*, ed. Alan Rudrum (New Haven, CT: Yale University Press, 1976), pp. 295–6.

22. Vaughan, pp. 246–7.

23. Vaughan, pp. 289–90.

24. Vaughan, p. 255.

25. Stevie Davies writes of Vaughan's profound indebtedness to Herbert and also notes the great difference in the two poets' circumstances: 'The earthly church as [Herbert] knew, praised and counselled it had been outlawed and its sacred architecture, from which he took his bearings, smashed. Vaughan was left alone with his Bible, the Book of Nature and the moodily chiaroscuro resources of his inner spirit'. *Henry Vaughan*, p. 102.

26. Thomas Traherne, *Selected Poems and Prose*, ed. Alan Bradford (London: Penguin, 1991), pp. 23–5.

27. Traherne, *Selected Poems and Prose*, p. 64.

28. Traherne, *Selected Poems and Prose*, p. 106.

29. Traherne, *Selected Poems and Prose*, p. 158.

30. Traherne, *Selected Poems and Prose*, p. 103.

31. Traherne, *Selected Poems and Prose*, p. 162.

32. Thomas Traherne, *Centuries* (New York: Harper & Brothers, 1960), pp. 36–7.

33. 'How was Anglican spirituality to develop out of this melting pot [of the seventeenth century]? It moved towards learning against piety, reason against affective feeling, transcendence against immanence, and landed in Deism' (Martin Thornton, 'The Caroline Divines and the Cambridge Platonists', p. 437).

34. 'Awake, my soul, and with the sun / Thy daily stage of duty run' and 'All praise to thee, My God, this night, / For all the blessings of the light.'

35. Ellen Davis dates this shift, at least in preaching, as far back as the reign of Charles II. 'For Andrewes, Hall, and Donne the sermon was a liturgical poem, a meditation on Scripture, a journey through Scripture into another world. For Tillotson, it was a moral essay, and the Bible a sourcebook of propositions about the moral life' (*Imagination Shaped*, p. 3).

36. Like Ken, Jennens was a non-juror, one of the party of strict Anglicans who refused to take the oath to William and Mary and their successors, and who formed a kind of parallel Church of England during the eighteenth century. They were a small group, but influential, since

they included in their number figures such as Bishop Ken and, later, William Law.

37. Pastiche was Jennens's real gift; he was also Handel's librettist for *Messiah*.

38. Text from the explanatory notes of recording of George Frideric Handel, *L'Allegro, il Penseroso, ed il Moderato*, as edited by John Eliot Gardiner (Musical Heritage Society, 1983).

39. See above, p. 153.

40. John Eliot Gardiner, explanatory notes for Handel's *L'Allegro, il Penseroso, ed il Moderato*.

41. Handel here seems to give a healing power to music that stands in sharp contrast to its destructive power, as portrayed just a few years before in his setting of Dryden's 'Alexander's Feast', where Dryden credits the destruction of Persepolis to the influence of the music of Timotheus.

42. Peter Holman, explanatory notes for William Boyce, *Solomon, A Serenata* (Hyperion, 1990).

43. *The Poems of Gray and Collins*, ed. Austin Lane Poole, 3rd edn, revised (London: Oxford University Press, 1937), pp. 91–7.

44. The *Elegy* probably reflects something of Gray's own temperament. Compare the wry 'Sketch of his own Character' written in 1761, eleven years after completion of the *Elegy*:

> Too poor for a bribe, and too proud to importune,
> He had not the method of making a fortune:
> Could love, and could hate, so was thought somewhat odd;
> No very great wit, he believed in a God:
> A place or a pension he did not desire,
> But left church and state to Charles Townshend and Squire.
>
> *The Poems of Gray and Collins*, p. 148.

45. Charles Wesley wrote of one collection of hymns: 'It is large enough to contain all the important truths of our most holy religion, whether speculative or practical; yea, to illustrate them all, and to prove them both by Scripture and reason': *John and Charles Wesley: Selected Prayers, Hymns, Journal Notes, Sermons, Letters and Treatises*, pp. 175–6.

46. *John and Charles Wesley*, pp. 176–7.

47. *John and Charles Wesley*, pp. 188–9.

48. *John and Charles Wesley*, p. 261. The banqueting house and banner allude to Song of Solomon 2:4.

49. William Cowper, 'Light Shining out of Darkness', lines 1–2, and 'Joy and Peace in Believing', lines 1–8 in *The Poetical Works*, ed. William Benham (London: Macmillan & Co., 1874), pp. 32, 38.

50. Alexander Pope, *An Essay on Man*.

51. T. S. Eliot described Blake as exhibiting 'the peculiarity of all great

poetry . . . a peculiar honesty, which, in a world too frightened to be honest, is peculiarly terrifying': *Selected Essays*, p. 275.

52. Edwin Mims quotes Alfred Kazin as saying, 'No Christian saint ever came to be more adoring of Jesus' (*The Christ of the Poets*, pp. 138–9).

53. *Blake's Poems and Prophecies*, ed. Max Plowman (London: J. M. Dent, Everyman, [1927] 1965), p. 18.

54. *Blake's Poems and Prophecies*, p. 15.

55. *Blake's Poems and Prophecies*, p. 23.

56. Wordsworth sent a copy of the new work to William Wilberforce, a leading evangelical reformer. R. L. Brett (*Faith and Doubt*, pp. 6–7) argues that both Wordsworth and Coleridge were profoundly influenced by Wilberforce's writing, even though Wordsworth, at least, 'had a marked dislike of the Evangelicals'.

57. William Wordsworth, *The Complete Poetical Works*, ed. Andrew J. George (Boston: Houghton Mifflin, 1904), pp. 91–3.

58. Wordsworth, *Complete Poetical Works*, p. 349.

59. Wordsworth, *Complete Poetical Works*, pp. 311–12.

60. *Samuel Taylor Coleridge*, ed. H. J. Jackson (Oxford: Oxford University Press, 1985), pp. 117–19.

61. *Biographia Literaria*, ch. xiii (Coleridge, p. 313).

62. Lay Sermons I (Coleridge, p. 661).

63. 'Kubla Khan', lines 49–54 (Coleridge, pp. 103–4).

64. Keble urged all who 'sincerely desire to understand and feel that secret harmonious intimacy which exists between honorable Poverty, and the severer Muses, sublime Philosophy, yea, even our most holy Religion' to read Wordsworth (quoted in R. L. Brett, *Faith and Doubt*, p. 36). See also A. M. Allchin in 'Anglican spirituality', p. 321.

65. John Keble, *The Christian Year: Thoughts in Verse for the Sundays and Holy Days throughout the Year* (New York: James Miller, Publisher, 1879), p. 14.

66. ' . . . the Tractarians were very much the heirs of the Lake poets. They owed to them their renewed sense of the sacramental quality of all things, the context in which their renewed apprehension of the meaning of the particular sacraments of the Church is to be placed' (A. M. Allchin, *The World Is a Wedding*, p. 42).

67. There are several references in the poems to others' disapproval of the length and intensity of his grief, e.g., vi, xxi, lxvi.

68. Alfred Tennyson, *In Memoriam* (Chicago: The Henneberry Company, n.d.), pp. 107–8.

69. Tennyson, *In Memoriam*, p. 108.

70. Tennyson, *In Memoriam*, pp. 47–8.

71. Tennyson, *In Memoriam*, pp. 112–13.

72. Tennyson, *In Memoriam*, pp. 83–4.

73. T. S. Eliot wrote, '*In Memoriam* can, I think, justly be called a religious poem, but for another reason than that which made it seem religious to his contemporaries. It is not religious because of the quality of its

faith, but because of the quality of its doubt. Its faith is a poor thing, but its doubt is a very intense experience' (*Selected Essays*, p. 294).

74. Tennyson, *In Memoriam*, p. 109.

75. Elizabeth Barrett Browning, *Poetical Works* (Chicago: Belford, Clarke & Co., n.d), pp. 62–5.

76. Line 7 alludes to the 'still small voice' heard by Elijah (1 Kings 19:9–18), though that voice has become a somewhat Wordsworthian voice heard in the natural world. The stanza also prepares the way for Barrett Browning's rejection of the popular Roman doctrine of the Virgin's immaculate conception in the following stanza – a rejection made not for polemical reasons here so much as in order to retain the voice of the Virgin as one that can speak for all humanity.

77. Christina Rossetti, *Poems and Prose*, ed. Jan Marsh (London: J. M. Dent, Everyman, 1994), p. 62.

78. Rossetti, *Poems and Prose*, pp. 31–5.

79. The stanza is dense with biblical allusion. The title of the poem comes from the crass complaint of Jesus' disciples in Matthew 26:8 (AV) when a woman anoints Jesus with 'very precious ointment'. The speaker's dream echoes the enthusiastic summons of the canticle *Benedicite* to every part of creation to join in the praise of God. More than that, the stanza alludes to the spirit of God (the Hebrew word for 'spirit' and 'wind' is the same) that hovered over the face of the waters in creation. This is the same Spirit that gives to each member of the church his or her own gift according to Paul in 1 Corinthians 12—14. Hence, the poet can treat the differing contributions of each element of creation as reflecting the same inspiration. The stanza concludes with allusions to Revelation 21 ('the walls of Heaven') and to Genesis 2 (Paradise).

80. Rossetti, *Poems and Prose*, p. 45.

81. The two men came from quite different churchly backgrounds, Dodgson being a deacon of evangelical persuasion and Lear a layman and a supporter (with his friends the Tennysons) of F. D. Maurice.

82. ' . . . the nonsense poem – if it works – refreshes us by surprise, by invention, or by commenting, in what is said or how it is said, on sense taking itself too seriously or being pompous, or in fashion': Geoffrey Grigson, in his introduction to *The Faber Book of Nonsense Verse*, p. 11.

83. Matthew Arnold, *Poetical Works*, ed. C. B. Tinker and H. F. Lowry (London: Oxford University Press, 1950), pp. 210–12.

84. But Arnold actually looked beyond the ethical. 'While self-denial and renouncement are spiritually essential, Arnold believed they are nevertheless only penultimate. For renouncement gives birth to resurrection, life, joy' (James C. Livingston, *Matthew Arnold and Christianity*, p. 172).

85. Arnold also wrote extensively on religious issues in prose. It is instructive that A. M. Allchin was able to use Arnold's prose as a

useful point of departure in his essay on 'Anglican spirituality', pp. 313–18.

86. Brett (*Faith and Doubt*, p. 192) suggests that two principles were at work here for Eliot: 'One is the belief he held at the time that in religion truth and meaning become one; it is pointless to attempt to verify historical facts, for what is important is the meaning the believer invests in them. The other is the importance he gave to mystical experience as an approach to the Absolute.'

87. The obscurity is in part an expression of the poetry's very intimacy. The poet speaks in a kind of private language, but one sufficiently connected to that of others as to provoke interest in what he may be saying through it. It has also become apparent that much of the content of *The Waste Land*, however well disguised, was intensely personal (Brett, *Faith and Doubt*, p. 191).

88. T. S. Eliot, *Collected Poems 1909–1962* (New York: Harcourt Brace & Co., 1964 and London: Faber & Faber, 1963), p. 187.

89. Eliot, *Collected Poems*, p. 185.

90. Brett (*Faith and Doubt*, p. 202) suggests that 'Eliot's interest in mysticism had given him an other-worldly disregard of the temporal, but the war and his participation in Christian discussions about the society likely to emerge from the conflict, led him to give greater importance to God's purpose in human history'. The shift is evident in *Four Quartets*. Brett also strongly credits the influence of Charles Williams and Reinhold Niebuhr.

91. Eliot, *Collected Poems*, p. 203.

92. Wilfred Owen, *The Poems*, ed. Jon Stallworthy (New York: W. W. Norton & Co., 1986 and New Directions Publishing Corporation, 1963), p. 192.

93. Owen, *Poems*, p. 159.

94. Owen, 'Sonnet: On Seeing a Piece of Our Heavy Artillery Brought into Action', lines 11–14 (*Poems*, p. 128).

95. John Betjeman, *Collected Poems*, enlarged edn, compiled by the Earl of Birkenhead (Boston: Houghton Mifflin Company, 1971), pp. 154–6.

96. W. H. Auden, *Collected Poems*, ed. Edward Mendelson (New York: Random House, 1976), pp. 559–60.

97. This move actually corresponds to the language of Acts 2:6, which emphasises the experience of the hearers.

98. Judith Wright, 'Two Songs for the World's End', lines 1–2, *Collected Poems 1942–1985* (Sydney: Angus & Robertson, 1994), pp. 107–8.

99. Wright, 'Good News', lines 41–7 (*Collected Poems*, pp. 334–5).

Prospect

1. Louis Glück, *The Wild Iris* (Hopewell, NJ: The Ecco Press, 1992).

2. I like A. M. Allchin's description of Henry Vaughan as 'an authoritative

witness to the wholeness and integrity of the Christian tradition' (*The World Is a Wedding*, p. 143).

3. 'Anglican spirituality', p. 322. There is one fleeting reference to George Herbert as poet in Stephen Neill, *Anglicanism*, 3rd edn, p. 227; and no separate treatment of the tradition in *The Study of Anglicanism*.

4. For the present, it is gay and lesbian people.

5. '... we should develop an approach in which the relating to God can be co-ordinated with views of nature and human beings, so that communion rather than isolation, adventure rather than passive conformity, risk rather than apathy, can be the hallmarks of the spiritual quest' (John E. Skinner, 'An incarnational spirituality', p. 142).

6. Elizabeth Clarke, 'George Herbert's *The Temple*: the genius of Anglicanism and the inspiration for poetry', pp. 127–30.

7. Paul Monette, *Love Alone: Eighteen Elegies for Rog* (New York: St Martin's Press, 1988).

8. Auden, 'Whitsunday in Kirchstetten', end, p. 560.

BIBLIOGRAPHIES

Poets

Matthew Arnold, *Poetical Works*, ed. C. B. Tinker and H. F. Lowry (London: Oxford University Press, 1950).

W. H. Auden, *Collected Poems*, ed. Edward Mendelson (New York: Random House, 1976 and London: Faber & Faber, 1976 and 1991).

Elizabeth Barrett Browning, *The Poetical Works*, 'From the last London edition' (Chicago: Belford, Clarke & Company, n.d.).

John Betjeman, *Collected Poems*, enlarged edn, compiled by the Earl of Birkenhead (Boston: Houghton Mifflin Company, 1971).

William Blake, *Blake's Poems and Prophecies*, ed. Max Plowman (London: J. M. Dent, Everyman, [1927] 1965).

Samuel Taylor Coleridge, *Samuel Taylor Coleridge*, ed. H. J. Jackson, The Oxford Authors (Oxford: Oxford University Press, 1985).

William Cowper, *The Poetical Works*, ed. William Benham (London: Macmillan & Co., 1874).

John Donne, *Devotions Upon Emergent Occasions*, ed. Anthony Raspa (New York: Oxford University Press, 1987).

John Donne, *The Complete Poetry and Selected Prose*, ed. Charles M. Coffin (New York: The Modern Library, 1952).

T. S. Eliot, *Collected Poems 1909–1962* (New York: Harcourt Brace & Company, 1964 and London: Faber & Faber, 1963).

Louise Glück, *The Wild Iris* (Hopewell, NJ: The Ecco Press, 1992).

Thomas Gray, *The Poems of Gray and Collins*, ed. Austin Lane Poole, 3rd edn rev. (London: Oxford University Press, 1937).

George Herbert, *The Country Parson, The Temple*, ed. John N. Wall, Jr, The Classics of Western Spirituality (New York: Paulist Press, 1981).

Robert Herrick, *The Poetical Works*, ed. F. W. Moorman (London: Oxford University Press, 1921).

Robert Herrick, *Robert Herrick*, ed. Douglas Brooks-Davies (London: J. M. Dent, Everyman 1996).

Gerard Manley Hopkins, *The Poems*, ed. W. H. Gardner and N. H. Mackenzie, 4th edn rev. and enlarged (London: Oxford University Press, 1970).

John Keble, *The Christian Year: Thoughts in Verse for the Sundays and*

Holy Days throughout the Year (New York: James Miller, Publisher, 1879).

Paul Monette, *Love Alone: Eighteen Elegies for Rog* (New York: St Martin's Press, 1988).

Wilfred Owen, *The Poems*, ed. Jon Stallworthy (New York: W. W. Norton & Company, 1986 and New Directions Publishing Corporation, 1963).

Christina Rossetti, *Poems*, selected Peter Washington, Everyman's Library Pocket Poets (New York: Alfred A. Knopf, 1993).

Christina Rossetti, *Poems and Prose*, ed. Jan Marsh (London: J. M. Dent, Everyman, 1994).

Christopher Smart, *The Collected Poems*, ed. Norman Callan, Vol. 1 (London: Routledge & Kegan Paul, 1949).

Stevie Smith, *A Selection*, ed. Hermione Lee (London: Faber & Faber, 1983).

Edmund Spenser, *Spenser's Minor Poems*, ed. Ernest de Sélincourt (Oxford: Clarendon Press, [1910] 1960).

Alfred Tennyson, *In Memoriam* (Chicago: The Henneberry Company, n.d.).

Alfred Tennyson, *The Poetic and Dramatic Works* (Boston: Houghton Mifflin Company, 1898).

R. S. Thomas, *Collected Poems 1945–1990* (London: Macmillan).

Thomas Traherne, *Centuries* (New York: Harper & Brothers, 1960).

Thomas Traherne, *Selected Poems and Prose*, ed. Alan Bradford (London: Penguin, 1991).

Henry Vaughan *The Complete Poems*, ed. Alan Rudrum (New Haven, CT: Yale University Press, 1976).

Charles Wesley, *John and Charles Wesley: Selected Prayers, Hymns, Journal Notes, Sermons, Letters and Treatises*, ed. Frank Whaling, The Classics of Western Spirituality (New York: Paulist Press, 1981).

William Wordsworth, *The Complete Poetical Works*, ed. Andrew J. George (Boston: Houghton Mifflin, 1904).

Judith Wright, *Collected Poems 1942–1985* (Sydney: Angus & Robertson, 1994).

Other Works

Allchin, A. M., *The World Is a Wedding: Explorations in Christian Spirituality* (New York: Oxford University Press, 1978).

Allchin, A. M., 'Anglican spirituality' in *The Study of Anglicanism*, ed. Stephen Sykes and John Booty (London: SPCK and Philadelphia: Fortress Press, 1988), pp. 313–25.

Avis, Paul, *Anglicanism and the Christian Church: Theological Resources in Historical Perspective* (Minneapolis: Fortress Press, 1989).

Booty, John, 'Contrition in Anglican spirituality' in *Anglican Spirituality*, ed. William J. Wolf (Wilton, CT: Morehouse-Barlow, 1982), pp. 25–48.

Brady, Veronica, *South of My Days: A Biography of Judith Wright* (Sydney: Angus & Robertson, 1998).

Brett, R. L., *Faith and Doubt: Religion and Secularisation in Literature from Wordsworth to Larkin* (Macon, GA: Mercer University Press, 1997).

Brooks-Davies, Douglas (ed.), *Robert Herrick*, Everyman's Poetry (London: J. M. Dent, 1996).

Bryant, Christopher, *The Heart in Pilgrimage: Christian Guidelines for the Human Journey* (New York: The Seabury Press, 1980).

Clarke, Elizabeth, 'George Herbert's *The Temple*: the genius of Anglicanism and the inspiration for poetry' in *The English Religious Tradition and the Genius of Anglicanism*, ed. Geoffrey Rowell (Nashville: Abingdon Press, 1992), pp. 127–44.

Davies, Stevie, *Henry Vaughan* (Bridgend, Wales: Seren, 1995).

Davis, Ellen, *Imagination Shaped: Old Testament Preaching in the Anglican Tradition* (Valley Forge, PA: Trinity Press International, 1995).

Eliot, T. S., *Selected Essays*, new edn (New York: Harcourt, Brace & Company, 1950).

Grigson, Geoffrey (ed.), *The Faber Book of Nonsense Verse* (London: Faber & Faber, 1979).

Guthrie, Harvey H., 'Anglican spirituality: an ethos and some issues' in *Anglican Spirituality*, ed. William J. Wolf (Wilton, CT: Morehouse-Barlow, 1982), pp. 1–16.

Jones, C. P. M., 'Mysticism, human and divine' in *The Study of Spirituality*, ed. Cheslyn Jones, Geoffrey Wainwright and Edward Yarnold (New York: Oxford University Press, 1986), pp. 17–24.

Lewalski, Barbara Kiefer, *Protestant Poetics and the Seventeenth-Century Religious Lyric* (Princeton: Princeton University Press, 1979).

Livingston, James C., *Matthew Arnold and Christianity: His Religious Prose Writings* (Columbia, SC: University of South Carolina Press, 1986).

Marsh, Jan (ed.), *Christina Rossetti: Poems and Prose* (London: J. M. Dent, Everyman, 1994).

Milbank, John, *The Word Made Strange: Theology, Language, Culture* (Oxford: Blackwell Publishers, 1997).

Miller, Perry, 'The plain style' in *Seventeenth-Century Prose: Modern Essays in Criticism*, ed. Stanley E. Fish (New York: Oxford University Press, 1971), pp. 147–86.

Mims, Edwin, *The Christ of the Poets* (New York: Greenwood Press, Publishers, 1969).

Neill, Stephen, *Anglicanism*, 3rd edn (Harmondsworth: Penguin Books, 1965).

Ricks, Christopher (ed.), *Tennyson: A Selected Edition* (Berkeley: University of California Press, 1989).

Runcie, Robert, 'Christian thinking: the Anglican tradition of thoughtful holiness', The Rita and William H. Bell Professorship in Anglican and

Ecumenical Studies: Public Lecture, The University of Tulsa, 8 April 1991.

Skinner, John E., 'An incarnational spirituality' in *Anglican Spirituality*, ed. William J. Wolf (Wilton, CT: Morehouse-Barlow, 1982), pp. 135–61.

Smalley, Susan J., 'Evelyn Underhill and the mystical tradition' in *Scripture, Tradition and Reason: A Study in the Criteria of Christian Doctrine*, Essays in Honour of Richard P. C. Hanson, ed. Richard Bauckham and Benjamin Drewery (Edinburgh: T. & T. Clark, 1988), pp. 266–87.

Strauss, Jennifer, *Judith Wright*, Oxford Australian Writers (Melbourne: Oxford University Press, 1995).

Summers, Joseph H., *The Heirs of Donne and Jonson* (New York: Oxford University Press, 1970).

Thomas, Frances, *Christina Rossetti* (London: Frances Thomas, with The Self Publishing Association, 1992).

Thornton, Martin, *English Spirituality: An Outline of Ascetical Theology According to the English Pastoral Tradition* (London: SPCK, 1963).

Thornton, Martin, 'The Caroline Divines and the Cambridge Platonists' in *The Study of Spirituality*, ed. Cheslyn Jones, Geoffrey Wainwright and Edward Yarnold (New York: Oxford University Press, 1986), pp. 431–7.

Wakefield, Gordon S., 'The Puritans' in *The Study of Spirituality*, ed. Cheslyn Jones, Geoffrey Wainwright and Edward Yarnold (New York: Oxford University Press, 1986), pp. 437–45.